The Homeowner Wealth Formula

Book #1 Of The

Homeowner Wealth Series

by Daniel R. Amerman, CFA

This book contain the ideas and opinions of the author. It is a conceptual exploration of financial and general economic principles. What this book does not contain is specific investment, legal, tax or any other form of professional advice. If specific advice is needed, it should be sought from an appropriate professional. Any liability, responsibility or warranty for the results of the application of principles contained in the book and related materials, either directly or indirectly, are expressly disclaimed by the author.

Copyright 2021 by Daniel R. Amerman

All rights are reserved.

ISBN: 978-1-7361175-0-7

The cover graphic is from Chapter 5, and shows the increase in median home prices in the U.S. between 1940 and 2019.

CONTENTS

Chapter 1
How Homes With Mortgages Have Created Wealth Over The Decades — 7

    A Natural Flow Of Wealth — 17
    Putting Together The Homeowner Wealth Formula — 19
    Turning Inflation Into Wealth — 24

Chapter 2
Home Prices, Inflation & Reversing The Flow Of Wealth — 27

    Three Ways Of Seeing Inflation — 28
    Ever More Dollars To Buy Everything — 33
    Home Prices & Inflation — 36
    The Relationship Between Home Prices & Inflation — 38
    A Core Source Of The Reliability Of The Homeowner Wealth Formula — 42

Chapter 3
How Inflation Compounds Homeowner Wealth — 47

    Creating Wealth With Compound Interest — 48

Inflation Is Compound Interest	52
Average Homeowner Experiences With Inflation	58
Inflation & The Natural Flow Of Wealth	65

Chapter 4
Turning Inflation Into Wealth With A Home & Mortgage 71

An Unequal Partnership	75
An Unequal Partnership Over Ten Years	80
The Historical Experience For All Ten Years	84
Playing Off An Artificial Intervention Against An Unequal Partnership To Create A Natural Flow Of Wealth	88
Why An 80% LTV Mortgage?	89

Chapter 5
The Long History Of Using Inflation & Homes To Multiply Wealth 95

A Stated Policy Of Destroying The Value Of Money	97
Aligning With The Government For A 10% Annual Gain	100
A History Of Halving & Doubling	102
The Longer Term National History Of A Wealth Creation Engine	108
Quaint Home Prices & Future Home Prices	118

Chapter 6
A 99.7% Chance Of Earning 5X The Money   121

Multiplying Very Low Rates Of Inflation	125
Five Times The Gain, 99.7% Of The Time	129
Increasing Reliability Over Time	131
A 100% Success Rate, With 5X The Wealth - But No Guarantees	132

Chapter 7
Turning High Inflation Into Rapid Wealth Creation   135

Three Times The Money In Three Years	137
Maximum Wealth Creation	141
Accidental Prosperity & Toy Mortgages	146

Chapter 8
Strengthening The Natural Flow Of Wealth With Amortization   151

How Amortization Works & Where It Leads	153
An Abundance Of Amortizations	158
High Interest Rates & Slow Amortizations	163
Low Interest Rates & Fast Amortizations	167
Looking Ahead With Contractual Amortizations	170

Chapter 9
The Homeowner Wealth Formula & The Nine High Stack   175

    Equity Gains That Build Fast   181

    Moving From 99.7% To 100% Wealth Drivers Safety   185

    Stacking Nine High With 100% Confidence   188

Book #2 Chapter Overview   193

    The Eight Levels Of Homeowner Wealth Multiplication   193

    Other Financial Education Resources   198

Author Information   199

Sources & Methodology Notes   203

Chapter 1

How Homes With Mortgages Have Created Wealth Over The Decades

About 65% of the households in the United States own the home they live in.

For these families and individuals, their single largest investment and their primary source of net worth is on average their equity in their home. According to the Federal Reserve's 2019 *Survey of Consumer Finances*, the median equity for those who own homes, the difference between the value of their home and their outstanding mortgage, is about $120,000. The median net worth for those same households is about $255,000.

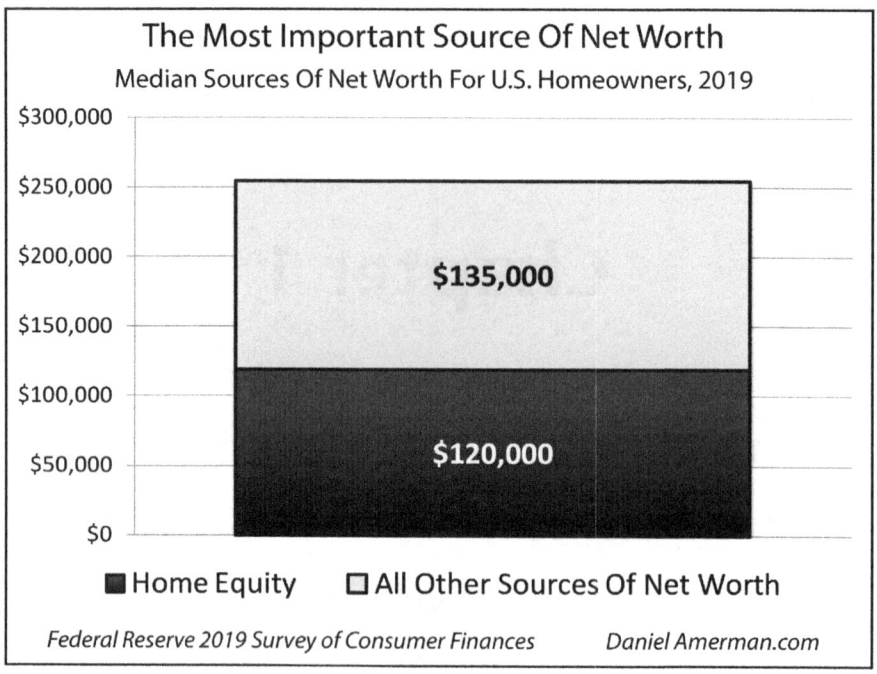

This means that for the average family with a home, almost half of their net worth is in their home equity. The value of their home equity is about as important for them as everything else put together including stocks, bonds, retirement accounts, life insurance and money in the bank.

Other than homes, the next largest source of net worth is retirement accounts. Looking just at retirement accounts (and not pensions), about half of U.S. households have retirement accounts, and the median value of those retirement accounts is about $65,000.

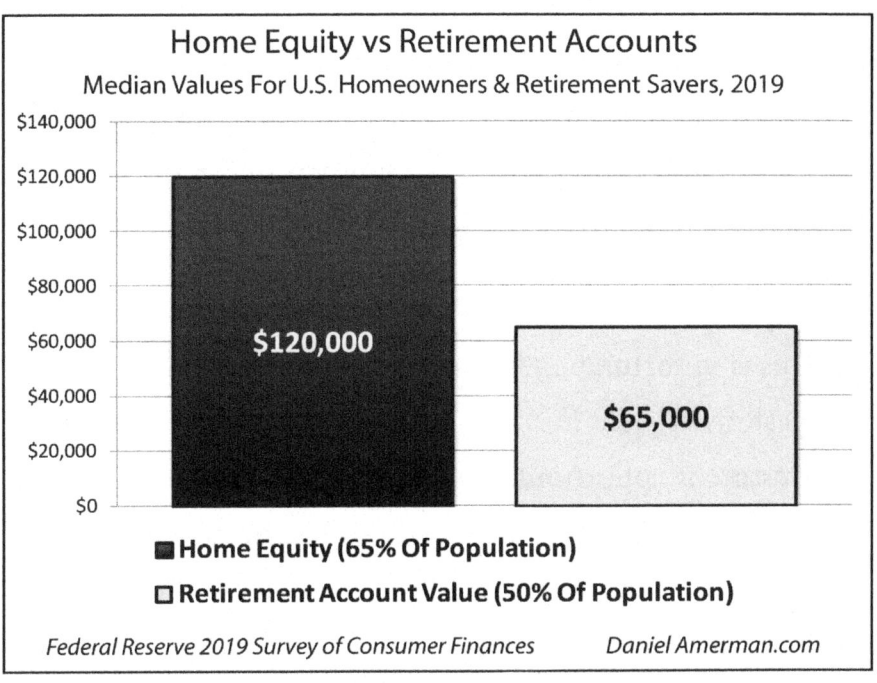

This means that if we look at an average American family, when comparing their home equity to their retirement account - *their homeownership is almost twice as financially important to them.*

The comparison is even more stark when we take into account that there are millions more homeowners, who are 65% of the nation's households, than there are retirement account owners, who are 50% of all households. The 15% difference represents millions of homeowners for whom their home equity is everything and their retirement account savings are zero.

There are a tremendous number of books, articles, classes and other forms of financial education out there when it comes to investing in stocks, bonds and retirement accounts. But yet, even though their home is by far their largest investment for most families, with a much larger contribution to their net worth than any stocks, bonds or retirement accounts they may own - there is comparatively little financial education available when it comes to investing in home ownership.

This is unfortunate - because homeownership is not only the largest investment for most people, it can also be the single best investment opportunity most people will ever have. Indeed, the single most reliable source of wealth creation for average American families over the decades has not been stocks, bonds or gold - but simply owning a single family home with a mortgage.

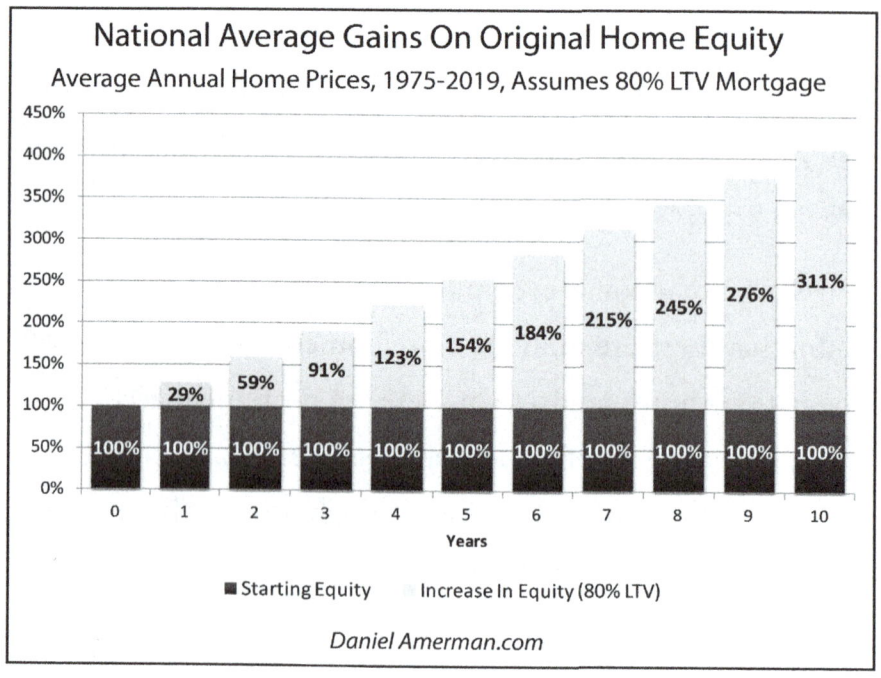

The average outcome for someone who purchased their home with an 80% loan to value (LTV) mortgage, and was in their home for three years - was to see their home equity almost double. Across the decades and for tens of millions of average homeowners, the collective homeownership experience was to keep their 100% starting equity and to see another 91% added, almost doubling their money in just three years.

The national average homeownership experience between 1975 and 2019 was for home equity to triple in the first seven years of owning a home.

If we go out to ten years, then *the national average experienced by the nation was for homeowners to see their home equity increase by more than four times,* for homes with 80% LTV mortgages.

If we want to understand how almost half the net worth of about two thirds of the population came to be in home equity - those numbers are why. The collective homeownership experience has been that - on average - to be a homeowner with a mortgage is to set in a motion a formula for building wealth via home equity that will grow to dominate all other sources of net worth.

These average homeownership experiences are not simply based on long term averages, but on almost four hundred individual analyses, of almost four hundred different homeownership periods.

What year someone bought, and how long they were in their home produced major differences over the decades - so the research behind this book is based on looking at the national averages for every possible 1 to 10 year homeownership period between 1975 and 2019, including the best years and the worst years.

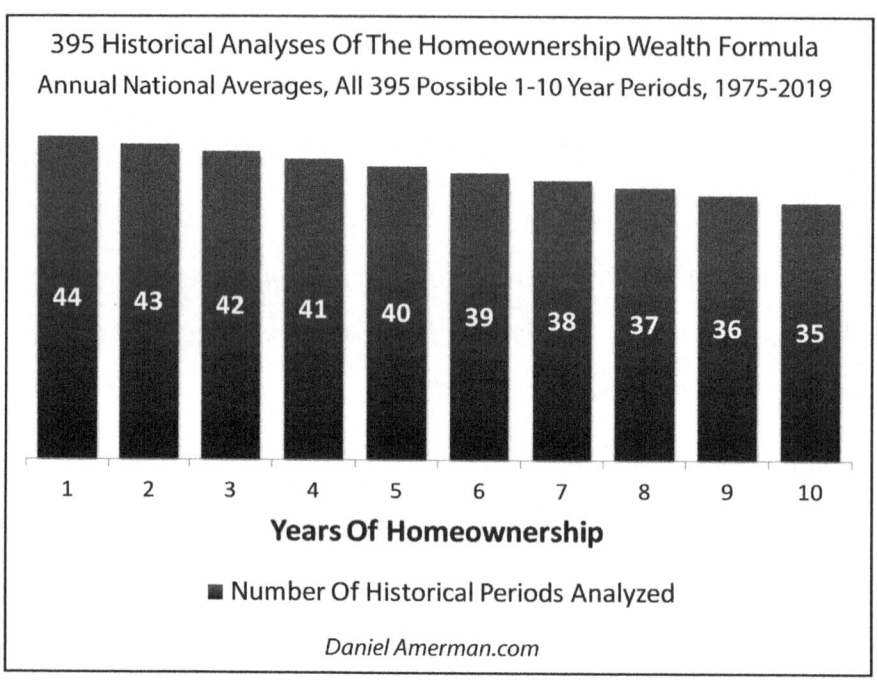

There were 42 possible three year ownership periods, ranging from 1975-1978 to 2016-2019. National average home price changes (and mortgage amortizations) for each three year period were individually analyzed, and when all 42 possibilities were averaged together - the average outcome for all the tens of millions of homeowners, across all the states and all those decades, was to see their home equity almost double.

For ten year homeownership periods, there were 35 of them, ranging from 1975-1985 through 2009-2019, and including every ten year period in-between. The national average homeowner experience was to see home equity quadruple in the first ten years of homeownership, assuming an 80% LTV mortgage was used to purchase the home.

What detailed analysis of decades of the average American homeownership experience proves is that a very powerful and unusually reliable flow of wealth is the natural result of simply being in the position of being a homeowner with a mortgage. It should also be noted that while the specific and detailed research is about homeownership in the United States, the results of the research and the general principles for creating wealth with a home and mortgage do apply to homeowners around the world.

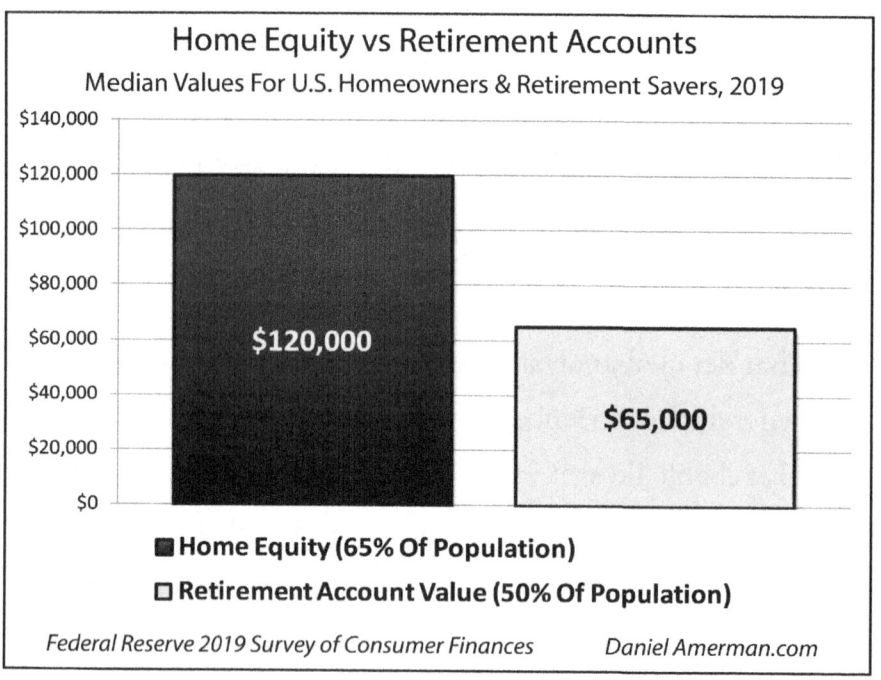

When we understand this natural flow of wealth, then the somewhat surprising relationship shown above becomes not just logical but expected. Setting up a retirement account is a matter of willpower and discipline. Consistently contributing to the retirement account with all that happens in life can be difficult. Becoming informed about and making good investment decisions for the retirement account is also not easy for many people.

In other words - every step can be difficult. Because each step is difficult, a lot of people don't set up retirement accounts, or consistently contribute to them, and even when they do - the national average amount of retirement savings is probably not as high as most would like it to be.

On the other hand, simply wanting to own and live in a nice place, perhaps a three bedroom home with a yard and a back deck, that is in a good school district - creates a natural flow of wealth that is itself a built in savings plan, even if that is not the reason why the home was purchased in the first place.

Making this much better is that homeownership comes with a natural formula for building wealth also built in, the Homeowner Wealth Formula, with that formula being the subject of this book.

When a homeowner is out in their garden, or entertaining on the patio, the natural result of being in that position is to have a wealth building machine creating net worth for them in the background. If there are children in the home, and they are at the ages where the family room floor is getting covered in toys - the natural result of owning that family room is to have entered into a surprisingly sophisticated and profitable investment strategy that can produce results that are almost impossible to get through most retirement account investments.

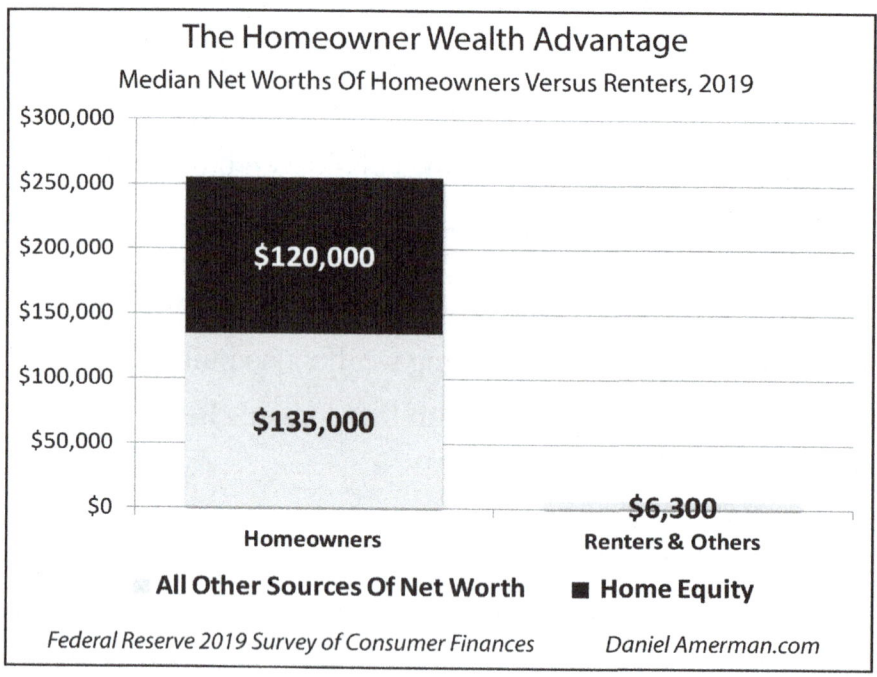

An even starker and almost shocking demonstration of the potentially life changing financial benefits of homeownership for the average person can be seen in the graph above. According to the Federal Reserve's 2019 *Survey of Consumer Finances,* the median net worth for the 65% of the population who are homeowners is $255,000, and the median net worth for the 35% who are renters (or other), is $6,300. The median is simply the household in the middle, where half of homeowners would have more and half would have less. When it comes to net worth - *the homeowner in the middle has a full 40X the net worth of the average renter.*

Now, it isn't all homeownership. The median income for homeowners is about $77,000 per year, and the median income for renters is about $36,000. Having a higher income helps a lot. But it doesn't explain the 40X difference, particularly when we look at how much of that difference is based on home equity.

Indeed with today's price levels, a $77,000 per year combined household income is not what it used to be, there is more to it than just the income difference. Consider two people, a renter and a homeowner, where the rent payment equals the mortgage payment. The renter pays rent - and it's gone for good. The homeowner uses the mortgage payment to access the ability to rapidly build wealth with the Homeowner Wealth Formula - and the average results for the nation can be seen above.

A Natural Flow Of Wealth

When most people think about making money with homes, whether as homeowners or investors, they think about making good purchases. Perhaps finding a particularly good property that is significantly underpriced. Maybe it is finding just the right neighborhood, where housing values are getting ready to take off.

On an individual basis - they are right. It is much better to buy a home in a good location at a low price, than to buy a home in a deteriorating neighborhood at a high price.

However, making good buys has nothing whatsoever to do with the extraordinary national averages for wealth creation that we just reviewed, instead they were the result of a natural flow of wealth.

What is a natural flow of wealth?

It is a matter of positioning, rather than of skill or of luck. So that the natural and average result of choosing to be in that position - of being a homeowner in this case - is to do well. Now, that is not the same thing as a guarantee, if someone turns out to be unusually bad at it, or turns out to be particularly unlucky then they can certainly lose, but a highly positive outcome is the natural and average result.

When we looked at home equity almost doubling in three years, or tripling in seven years, or quadrupling in ten years - those were just the averages, nothing special. There was no great skill, or luck, or working through elaborate financial charts or timing strategies. Those weren't just the good neighborhoods or only the most astute home buyers - those were all the buys, all the above average results and all the below average results combined, over all the decades and the regions of the nation.

Now some people are skillful, some people are lucky, and a fortunate few are both. With good skill or good luck - being smart and picking just the right property, or being in just the right area, or owning during a time when national home prices are doing unusually well - can produce potentially much, much better results than the simple long term national averages shown above.

Another feature of a natural flow of wealth is that it should be forgiving. There should be a wide range for experiencing below average results, and still being just fine. So, if someone's homeownership experience in practice works out to be in the bottom quarter or third of the national averages - as it will for 25% to 33% of homeowners over a long enough time period - it should still be, if not quite as good as average, still pretty good or at least OK. That is the case with homeownership, there is a very strong positive skew, that gets stronger and stronger over time.

Putting Together The Homeowner Wealth Formula

For the average person, homeownership will be the single most important financial or investment decision they will make in their lives.

For the average person, buying a home with a mortgage will be the single best investment decision they will make in their lives.

Those are a couple of fairly strong statements - but the evidence is overwhelming. As introduced in this chapter, and then explained and developed in the rest of the book, the history of homeownership over the decades is one of extraordinary average results when it came to rapid wealth creation and the reliability of that wealth creation.

These historical results can then essentially be confirmed from an entirely different source when we just look at the financial situation of the average (meaning median in this case) American today, as captured in the Federal Reserve's definitive once every three year *Survey of Consumer Finances.*

Home equity is almost half of their net worth for the 65% of the nation's households that are homeowners. Home equity is almost twice as important as retirement accounts, when it comes to net worth. The median homeowner has an astonishing 40X the net worth of the median renter.

But yet, ironically, the sources of that wealth are generally poorly understood, even by the very people who have financially benefited from 10, 20 or 30 years of homeownership. The bookshelves are full of financial education resources about retirement accounts, stocks, bonds, mutual funds and ETFs, as is the daily media - but there is comparatively little about a source of net worth that will in practice be almost twice as financially important as retirement accounts for the average person building wealth over the long term.

Financial history is quite clear that the best way of building wealth over the long term is not adding money but multiplying money. There are eight different levels of the multiplication of wealth that come as the natural result of owning a home that was purchased with the aid of a mortgage. Each level of multiplication is important. Multiplying money is better than adding money. And eight multiplications is much better than one multiplication.

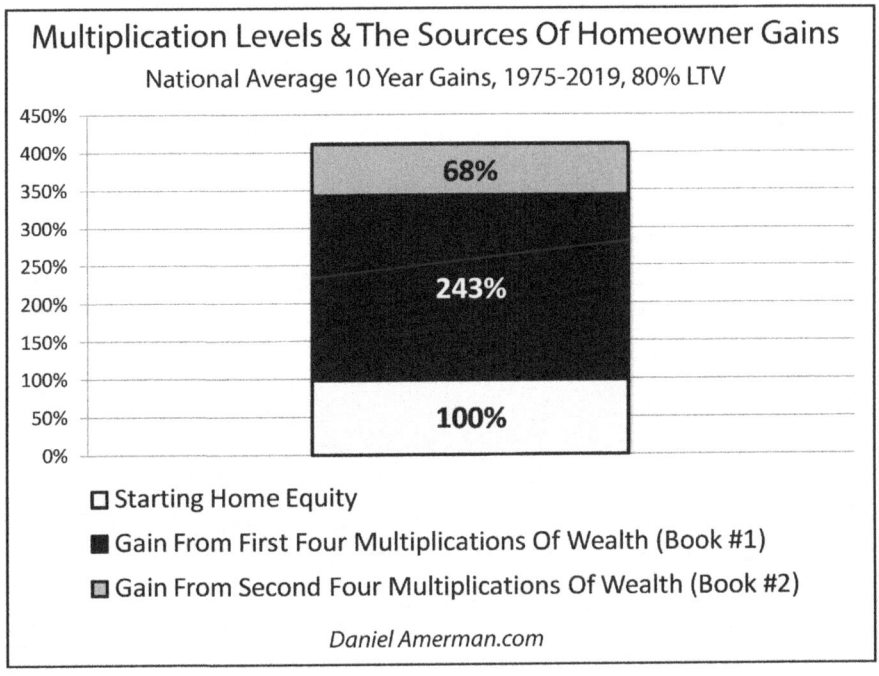

The first four levels of the multiplication of wealth are the subject of this Book #1 in the series. They are the most important, and the most reliable of the multiplications. The national average outcome for ten years of homeownership is to see home equity increase by 4.1X, of which 3.4X are the result of the first four levels of multiplication.

The remaining about 0.7X increase in home equity is the result of the second four levels of multiplication, which are the subject of Book #2 in this series.

The starting point for understanding where the multiplied wealth really comes from and why it has been so reliable for so many millions of homeowners over the decades, is that the main underlying wealth creation engine is not real market value changes - but inflation.

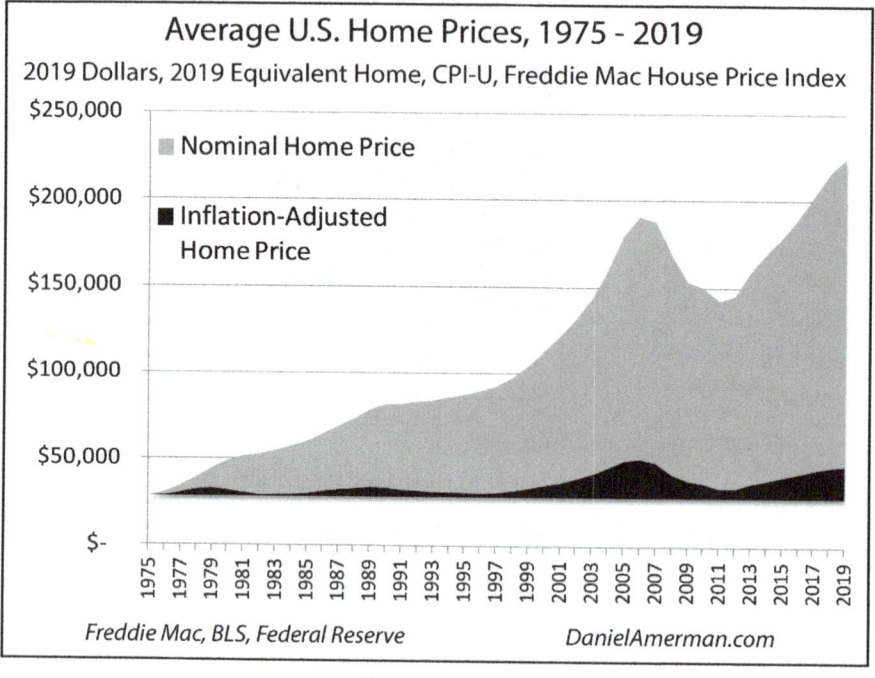

According to the Federal Reserve, the median value of the American home was $225,000 in 2019. Using the Freddie Mac House Price Index, a comparable home in 1975 (same size and amenities as in 2019), would have cost about $28,500.

When we adjust for inflation, then equivalent homes in 2019 were valued about 67% more highly than in 1975, and the real market value of the home would be up to about $47,400.

The other $177,600 increase in the price of the home? It's all inflation. So, the national average over 44 years was for the real price of a home to increase by $18,900, while inflation would increase it by almost ten times that, or $177,600. Over shorter time periods inflation is not as dominant - but it was still by far the largest creator of homeowner wealth when we look at all 395 of the national homeownership experiences.

Everyone focuses on trying to anticipate changes in housing market values, and sure they are important, but the historical evidence is overwhelming that inflation is where the real money comes from for the homeowners of the nation, most of the time. The true primary source of half of the net worth of most homeowners is not based upon the vagaries of changes in market values, but one of the most reliable financial forces in the world, which is the U.S. government's determination to create inflation and thereby destroy at least part of the value of the dollar in each and every year.

Chapters 2 & 3 will explore the close relationship between inflation, home prices and the compound interest formula. Just by themselves, for most people these chapters may be enough to change the way they look at homeownership, how they can rapidly build financial security, what their risks are, and the actual source of what could be half or more of their future net worth.

Turning Inflation Into Wealth

Keeping up with inflation is very good, it is highly desirable in comparison to many other types of investments, and that by itself is enough to place homeownership into the rarified territory of inflation hedges such as gold and silver. However, when a home is purchased with a mortgage, then something much rarer and much more powerful is created.

Homes with mortgages have an outstanding historical track record for *turning inflation into wealth*. In this case, home equity doesn't just keep up with inflation, instead it turns that inflation into wealth, where new home equity is created at a rate that can be much faster than the rate of inflation.

This powerful source of wealth creation is a very nice source of net worth over time even with quite low 1% to 2% annual rates of inflation. It works much better and more rapidly in creating wealth with moderate 3% - 4% annual rates of inflation. With high rates of inflation - owning a home with a mortgage is arguably the best protection against inflation that an ordinary person can obtain. The higher the rate of inflation, then the more rapidly wealth is created, and the greater the degree to which home equity and financial security grow faster than the rate of inflation.

This is the natural result of owning a home with a mortgage. If we want to understand why the median homeowner has 40X the net worth of the median renter - it is this highly reliable wealth creation engine chugging away beneath the surface, steadily turning inflation into wealth, that has been the primary driver of increases in home equity. As we will be reviewing, this isn't theory or guesses about the future - but is instead what has actually happened in practice for generations of homeowners (possibly including the reader and/or the reader's parents and grandparents).

Even by the time that Chapters 4 & 5 are completed and the first three levels of the multiplication of wealth are understood, the reader will have a good grasp of a very powerful and entirely different way of steadily creating wealth over the years, *that is not part of the usual consumer financial education.* This new and practical understanding will be reinforced and expanded in each succeeding chapter.

For the average person - choosing to own a home with a mortgage will be the most important financial decision of their lifetime, and this is true whether they understand the underlying wealth creation process or not. By the time this book is completed, readers should indeed understand this remarkable natural flow of wealth that can transform their lives - and hopefully be able to make better life and financial decisions as a result of that understanding.

Let's begin in the next chapter with three different ways of looking at inflation, and learn why the approach that is the least followed by the general public - is the foundation for what history shows us may be the single best investment that the average person will ever make.

Chapter 2

Home Prices, Inflation & Reversing The Flow Of Wealth

Inflation is one of the strongest financial forces in existence, and it is usually a powerful negative flow of wealth for individuals. Inflation is a wealth destroyer, as it takes ever more money to buy the same things. This means that cash will buy less each year, as will savings, as will bonds. The same destruction of purchasing power applies to salaries that don't keep up with inflation, as well as annuities and pensions, and this means that inflation can create impoverishment over time for many people.

Inflation is also one of the most powerful components of the homeowner wealth formula, indeed, it is the core source of most of the profitability and most of the reliability of the financial benefits of homeownership. This is because, as will be developed in this and the following chapters, a homeowner with a mortgage is naturally in a position to do something that is usually almost impossible for an average person to do - they can reverse the usual flow and turn inflation into wealth. Indeed, the higher the rate of inflation, the more real wealth that is created for the homeowner.

Three Ways Of Seeing Inflation

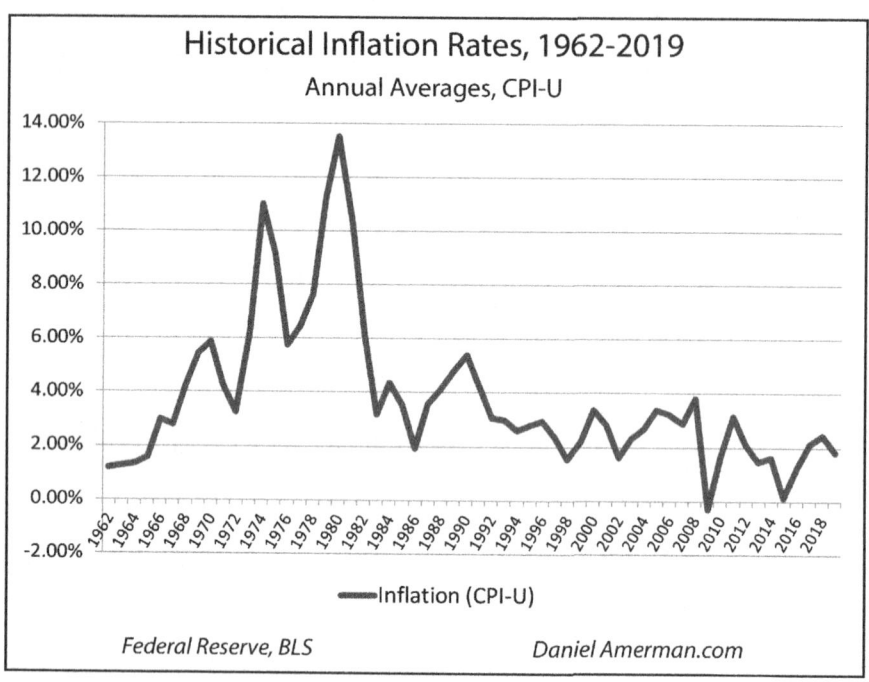

The first way of looking at inflation is the annual rate of inflation, which is what is usually reported in the media. The graph above shows annual rates of inflation since 1962 as reported by the U.S. government. The particular inflation measure shown is the Consumer Price Index (CPI-U), which is by far the most commonly reported inflation index.

The CPI-U is intended to measure increases in the cost of living on an average basis for urban consumers across the United States. So if we look at everything that someone might buy from groceries to haircuts to gasoline to rent, if those go up by an average of 4% for a typical person, then the rate of inflation is reported to be 4%.

The graph also helps to illustrate a couple of key considerations for the homeowner wealth formula, and how it has created wealth for so many millions of people. The first consideration is that annual rates of inflation have been highly variable over the years.

Homeowners experienced very high rates of inflation in the 1970s and 1980s, and then much lower rates of inflation in the 2000s and 2010s. This means that the sources of wealth for homeowners worked quite differently during the two time periods.

The second key point is that not everything in the graph is random. Instead, much of the inflation has been created as a matter of government policy.

The Federal Reserve, which is the central bank for the United States, sets the monetary policy for the nation. As a matter of policy for many decades, the Federal Reserve has set a target inflationary rate that has usually been in the range of around 2% a year (as have other central banks around the world).

Inflation is no accident - far from it. Creating an inflation rate of somewhere around 2% per year is openly stated government policy. The theory is that a low rate of inflation is beneficial for economic growth and full employment.

Whether that theory is correct or not is more or less irrelevant for savers and homeowners. The Federal Reserve believes in the theory, it is determined to see the value of money fall by at least a little bit every year, and it will use every bit of its extraordinary powers to make sure that our dollars will purchase less this year than last year, and will purchase still less next year, and then still less the year after.

What that means is that if we define "natural" not as being the laws of nature, but the way that the nation's economic and financial system are set up, then inflation is an enormously powerful force that creates a natural flow that is the steady destruction of the purchasing power of our money, year after year after year.

For someone who is fighting this force, who goes into opposition in order to try to hang on to the value of what they have, this becomes a lifetime struggle against an enormously powerful opponent - where the natural result, using the most common consumer savings and investment tools, is to steadily lose the fight.

On the other hand, for those using alternative strategies that financially benefit from this powerful natural flow, then their wealth is increased every year as the natural result of this ongoing process. And if control is lost every now and then, and inflation surges well above the Fed's targeted inflation rates - then that much more financial benefit flows through to those people, and it happens that much faster.

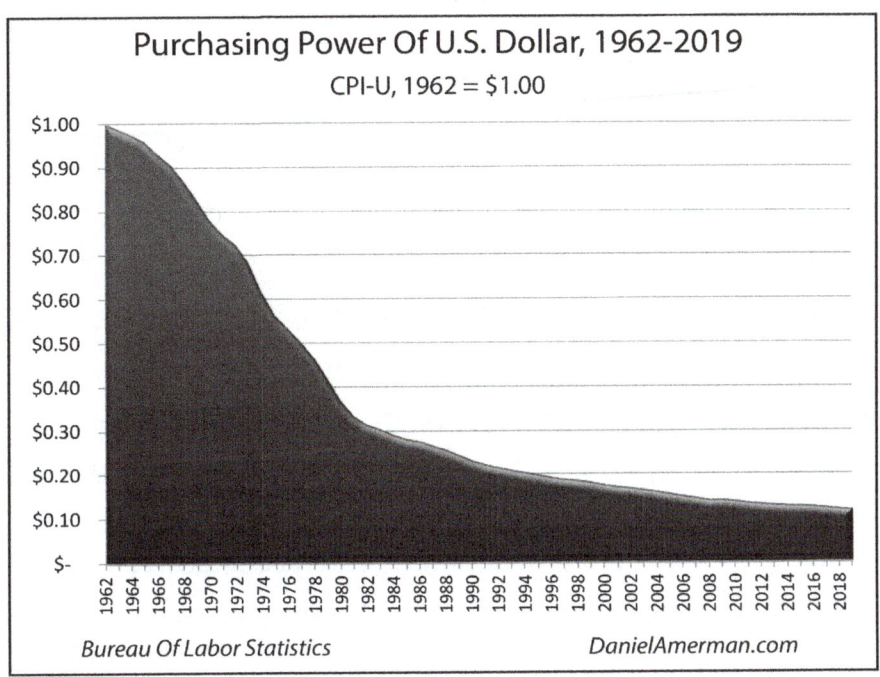

Another way of looking at inflation is not as an annual percentage, but in terms of what really matters over time, which is the steady, relentless and cumulative destruction of the purchasing power of the U.S. dollar.

The above graph shows the purchasing power of the dollar between 1962 and 2019. This is a cumulative process. If the dollar drops to being worth 95 cents in one year, then its starting point for the next year is 95 cents. And if it drops in value by 5% in that year, then it ends up being worth only 90 cents on the dollar, compared to where it was 2 years before. This steady process - that is a matter of explicit government policy - means that even with what may seem to be relatively low rates of inflation, there is still a steady, cumulative destruction that is effectively a one-way street, and becomes ever more powerful over time.

The purchasing power of the dollar dropped in half between 1962 and 1977. It then dropped in value by about half again, between 1977 and 1988, meaning a dollar only purchased about 25 cents in 1988 compared to where it had purchased in 1962. The dollar then dropped in value by about half again between 1988 and 2016, meaning that a dollar only had twelve and a half cents of purchasing power left compared to what it had been a little more than 50 years before.

Now, a lot of that destruction in purchasing power was an accident when inflation slipped out of control between the late 1960s and the mid 1980s. But not most of it, particularly if we look at the 1975 to 2019 era where we have good data on home prices. The average annual rate of inflation between 1975 and 2019 was 3.6%. The usual goal for the Federal Reserve during times of general price stability is to try to destroy on average around 2% of the value of the dollar - and the value of the average person's savings - each year.

This means that more than half of the cumulative destruction of purchasing power of the dollar - is entirely intentional. It is a "natural" force, where over the course of our lifetimes the government will do its absolute and relentless best to make sure that the dollar is worth at least a little bit less every year, quite a bit less every five years, and a lot less every ten years.

Economic history also shows us that much higher rates of inflation happen again and again over the centuries for nations with paper currencies (not backed by gold, silver or other tangible assets). Those types of inflation are another natural force, from another source, that also acts to destroy the value of money and sometimes at speeds that are much greater than governments might wish. The two forces, desired inflation and undesired inflation, do not offset, but rather combine to force the purchasing power of money down that much faster.

Ever More Dollars To Buy Everything

The third way of looking at inflation is the least common for the general public, but it is the underlying source of all the numbers, and it has a very direct applicability for the homeowner wealth formula.

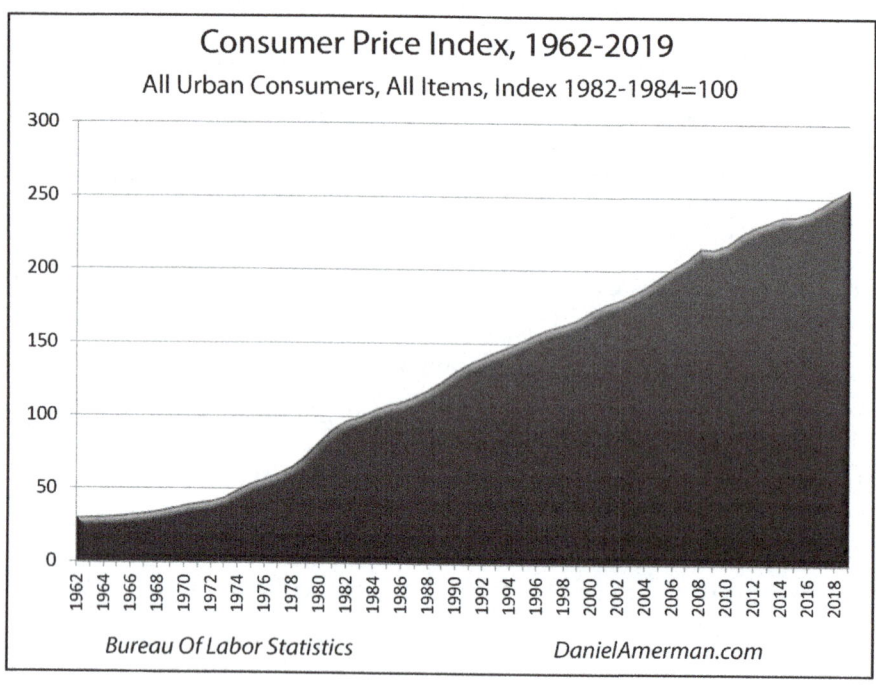

We get inflation when something increases, not when it decreases, and inflation is a measure of rising price levels. The consumer price index reflects how much more money it takes each year to buy a given basket of goods and services, which is supposed to reflect the cost of living for the average urban consumer. So as shown in the graph, the consumer price index steadily rises in each year, as it takes more and more money for the average person to maintain their lifestyle.

When we look at the consumer price index, we still have a relentless, unstoppable, one way process, where more than half of what we have experienced since 1975 is an entirely deliberate matter of governmental policy, with the Federal Reserve using its enormous powers over the value of money itself to try to make sure that inflation occurs.

However, instead of the relentless and cumulative destruction of purchasing power, there is the relentless and cumulative expansion (i.e. inflation) of the number of dollars, as it takes ever more money to buy the components of an average standard of living.

So, we can reverse our prior example of halving the purchasing power of dollars, and instead double the quantity of dollars, in a steady, cumulative and never ending process.

Consumers paid twice the money to buy everything (on average) in 1977 than they did in 1962. They then paid twice the money again to buy everything in 1988, meaning they paid four times the money relative to 1962. Consumers then paid twice the money again to buy their lifestyles by 2016, meaning they paid eight times the money that they would have paid in 1962.

Indeed, while little remarked upon, the mathematical formula for inflation is identical to the mathematical formula for compound interest. The first doubling sets the base for the second doubling, that sets the base for the third doubling, as the money gained each year comes in faster than the year before, in an exponential progression, whether it is interest on interest, or inflation on inflation.

Crucially, what we need to keep in mind about this relentless process of paying ever more dollars each year to buy the same things, in a cumulative manner that just builds and grows ever more powerful with each passing year - is that those dollars are being paid to someone else who is selling. Now, if that owner who was selling - or least looking at market value if they did sell - had bought the asset years before, then the owner would be fully benefiting from the process of inflation.

For an asset owner in that position, then inflation would represent a relentless, cumulative and one way process of feeding ever more money to them. Every year, as the government used its full powers to increase the money that it takes to buy a given standard of living - the government would also be acting to increase the amount of money the asset would sell for. If inflation were to soar out of control, then the amount of money others would be willing to pay for the asset would also be leaping upwards at a far faster rate, soaring with the rate of inflation - and never coming back down.

Could homes be such an asset? Let's check that out.

Home Prices & Inflation

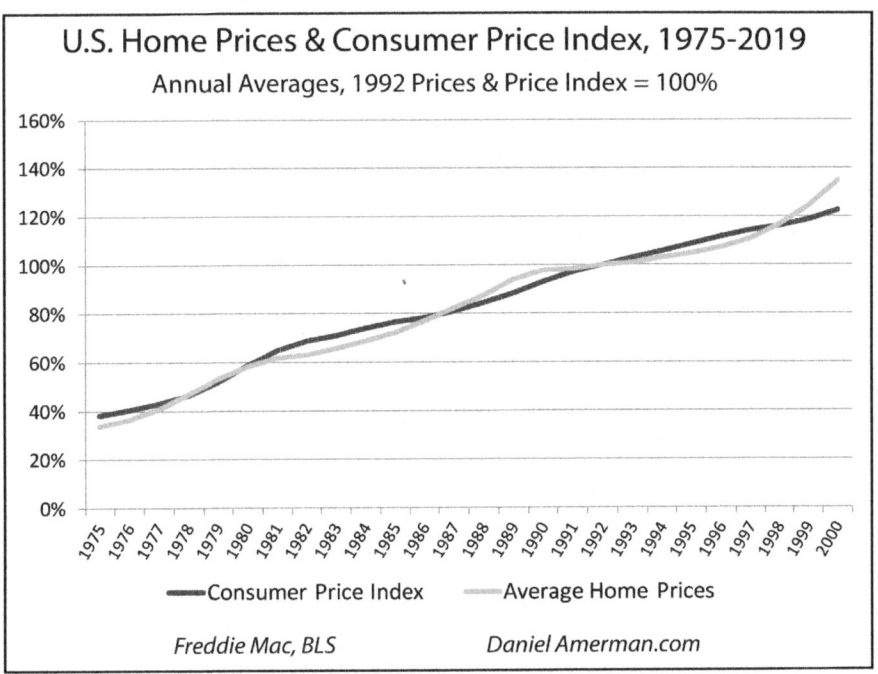

The two lines in the graph are U.S. home prices and the consumer price index between 1975 and 2000 (we will more closely focus on 2001 to 2019 in Book #2). As can be readily seen - housing prices and inflation track together almost perfectly, the lines can be hard to separate.

Home prices increased in a manner that was almost identical to the increases in the consumer price index. Each year that it took more money to pay for an average standard of living - it took a very similar percentage increase in money to buy the then average home.

Something else to keep in mind is that the relationship was steady, even as the amount and sources of inflation went through a number of stages, that were quite different from each other. The consumer price index and national average U.S. home prices tracked almost perfectly during the 1970s and early 1980s when inflation was raging out of control - meaning home prices were rising almost in lockstep with inflation.

Yet, they also tracked very closely through the 1990s, when inflation had been tamed and brought down into the 2%-4% range, and most inflation was the result of deliberate government policies.

The Relationship Between Home Prices & Inflation

Why should housing prices be tied to inflation?

One good explanation is that there has historically been a strong relationship between the prices of existing homes, and the costs of building new homes. The cost of a new home is the land, the sum of all the materials it takes to build it, and the labor to put everything together.

All of those prices for wood, shingles, drywall, windows, plumbing, and wiring, as well as all the contractors and labor to put them together, tend to naturally rise at least a bit each year as the natural byproduct of government policies to increase the number of dollars that it takes to buy most things by around 2%

each year. And when inflation jumps above government goals, as it can do for long periods of time, then the costs of building a new home can jump up by much more than 2% a year.

This creates a two-sided self-correcting mechanism that acts to keep home prices in line with inflation, so long as A) undeveloped land is available within a reasonable commuting distance of where the work is; and B) regulatory burdens are not excessive.

If home prices climb faster than the rate of inflation - then builders have a major financial incentive to build new homes, because they can build homes for significantly cheaper than what they can sell them for, and they can put the difference in their pockets. So the supply of homes rapidly increases until it exceeds the demand for homes, and this either brings home prices down or at least keeps them from increasing. Equilibrium is then reached, and builders no longer have the ability to earn excess profits from new construction.

In other words over the entire nation, home builders seeking profits are a price correction mechanism that historically kept national average housing prices from increasing too much faster than the rate of inflation.

On the other hand, if home prices do not keep up with the rate of inflation, then builders can't sell new homes for what it costs to build them. So they stop building, in order to avoid taking a loss on each home that they build. The population continues to increase, the supply of homes does not, this means that demand exceeds supply, a shortage develops, home prices rise until they reach the point where builders can once again profitably build homes, and a supply of new homes returns to the market.

Restated, for the nation, home builders avoiding losses are a price correction mechanism that historically kept national average home price increases from dropping too much below the rate of inflation.

Put the two together, and a relatively tight band is created.

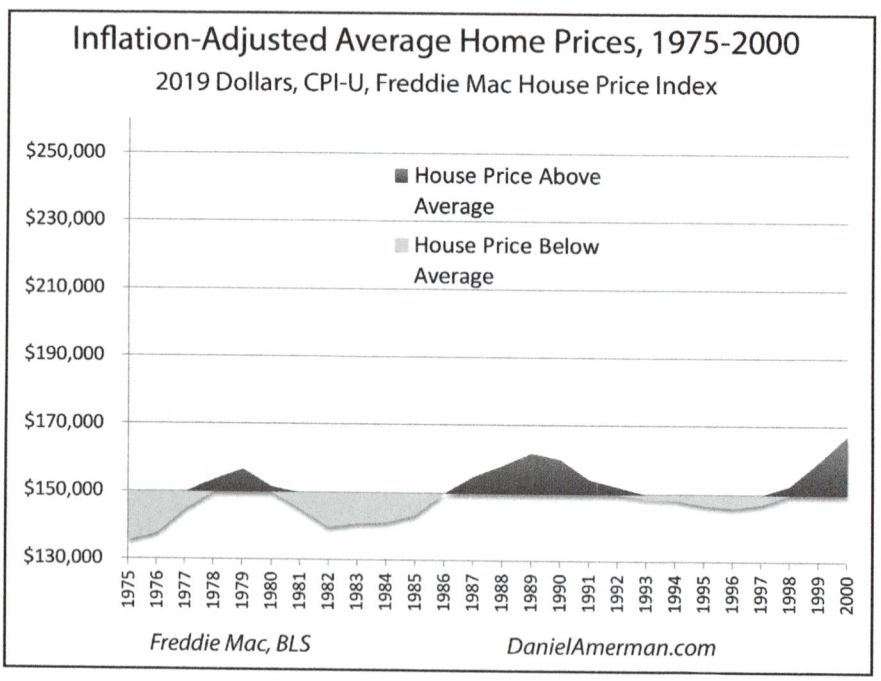

When we look not at the total dollars, but the purchasing power of the dollars, and look at national average home prices in inflation-adjusted terms before 2001 in the graph above (using 2019 dollars), then we see a very tight band indeed over the years. Home prices never went more than 10% below their long term inflation-adjusted average price over those years, and they never went more than 11% above their long term average price.

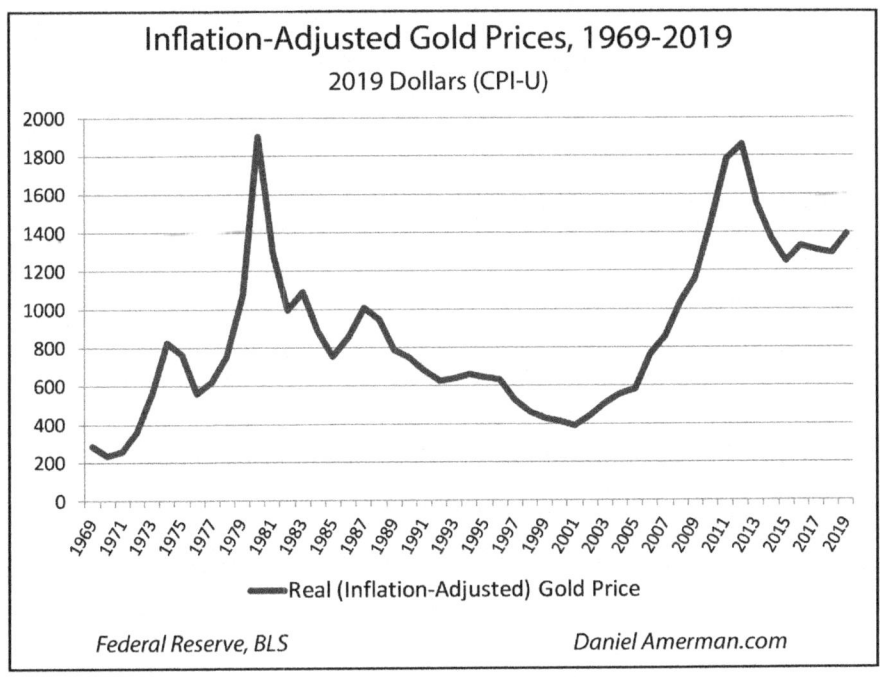

That is remarkably close relationship, and it is worth noting that single family homes have actually had a much closer relationship with inflation in practice than even gold prices, which have soared up and down over time, as shown on the graph and covered in more detail on my website.

Because this relationship between home prices and inflation was so close for so many years, it meant that the great majority of the changes in home prices on a national average basis could be explained by changes in inflation.

And inflation isn't random.

A Core Source Of The Reliability Of The Homeowner Wealth Formula

This changes everything. Indeed, this purposeful lack of randomness is the heart of why owning a home with a mortgage has been such a reliable creator of so much wealth for so many millions of families over the decades.

Whether someone wins or loses in a casino is random, but with the odds favoring the house. Whether someone wins or loses playing the state lottery is random, but with the odds favoring the state government(s).

In academic theory, investment prices are supposed to reflect all of the best available information at any point in time. This means that it is supposed to be more or less of a "random walk" whether a given share of stock we might buy goes up or down next week, over the next year, or over the next ten years (but with the odds favoring the "house" over time in the form of Wall Street and the financial industry).

Even for the stock market as a whole, over the long term it is not that uncommon for the stock market to take major losses over the period of ten years or more, particularly when we look at prices in inflation-adjusted terms.

Homes are different.

Creating at least a low to moderate rate of inflation is a matter of explicit governmental policy, and the Federal Reserve uses its vast powers over the banking industry and the very nature of money itself to try to make sure that money will buy at least a little less every year than it did year before.

History shows that the Fed is very, very good at doing this, they almost always succeed.

The Federal Reserve creates a steady and relentless destruction of the value of the dollar that is a lifetime challenge for savers, and that can be very difficult to stay ahead of, particularly on an after-tax basis.

The Fed accomplishes this by doing everything they can to make sure that it takes more dollars to buy everything each year. And that means - on a national average basis - the government is doing everything it can to make sure that more dollars must be spent in order to buy homes every year.

This destruction of the purchasing power of the dollar is a cumulative, one way street.

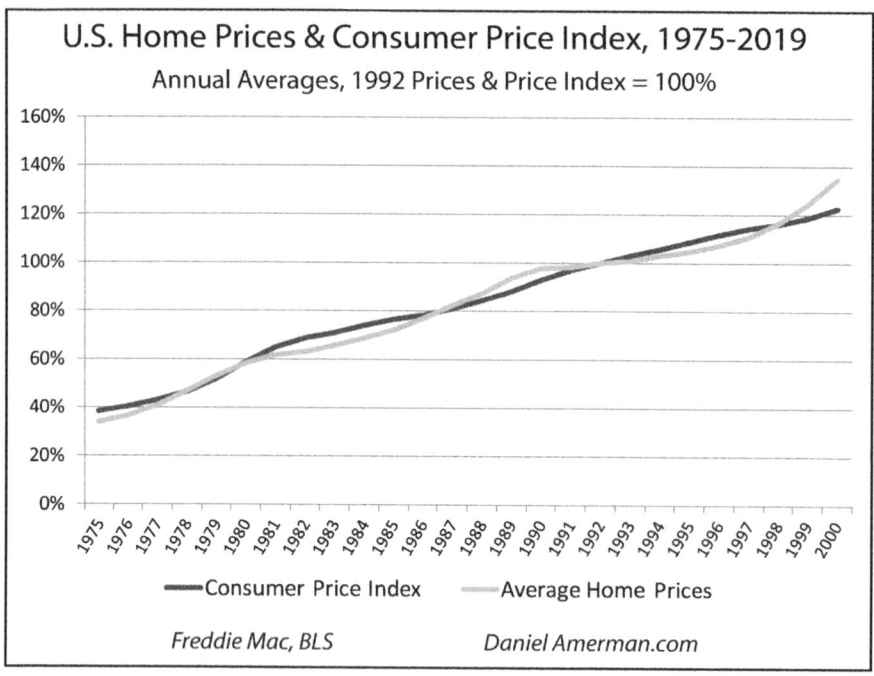

As can be seen in the graph repeated above, the number of dollars that it took to pay for an average standard of living doubled between 1975 and 1985, and tripled between 1975 and 1997. There weren't big, random swings up and down, but a relentless, cumulative process, where inflation built on inflation that built on inflation, much like compound interest builds on compound interest.

The home price line isn't identical - but it is really close. Home prices for equivalent homes almost exactly tracked what was happening with overall inflation, and that meant that across the nation, the amount of dollars that had to be paid to buy an average home about doubled between 1975 and 1985, and about tripled between 1975 and 1997.

This is the first level of the multiplication of wealth, the multiplication of the dollars needed to buy homes with each year of inflation.

These steady and over time soaring increases in home prices were not random, but a matter of alignment with both the "natural" flow of wealth created by government policies, and the "natural" flow of wealth that is created when inflation slips its bounds and goes too high. Home prices followed a relentless, cumulative, one way path that went ever upwards, with ever more money being required to buy homes - and ever more equity and value being created for existing homeowners.

(Those with education in finance and economics may be reading this chapter and saying "Ok, but what about inflation-adjusted purchasing power? An increase in nominal dollars where each dollar is worth less does not necessarily mean more wealth in real dollars." All I can say is wait two chapters for when we add a mortgage, and then things will develop.)

Chapter 3

How Inflation Compounds Homeowner Wealth

The most reliable way of making money over time is not to add money - but to multiply money. Saving a given amount out of each paycheck adds up over time, but that is all it does - it adds up. Now, adding up savings over time is a wonderful idea for building personal financial security, but by itself, it can be a very slow process.

For instance, if someone saves $1,000 and puts it in their retirement account, and they have no investment earnings, then their investment will still be equal to $1,000 in ten years. They will also have the same $1,000 in twenty years, in thirty years and in forty years.

If they are disciplined savers and they save $1,000 every year for ten years, then they have $10,000. If they work hard and save for forty years - then they have $40,000.

Those savings are great, they provide a tremendous increase in financial security - but getting them was not easy. The money had to be earned, taxes needed to be paid, bills needed to paid, and there needed to be consistent financial discipline in every year, through good times and bad, to find the extra money to steadily build those savings.

This process is also known as "our working for our money", and in theory it is something everybody should be doing - but in practice it is difficult for a lot of people to do. If we want to understand why the Federal Reserve's 2019 Survey of Consumer Finances found that only about half of all households have retirement accounts, and why the median value of those accounts was "only" about $65,000 - that is exactly why. The goal is highly desirable, but the process of getting there can be hard work over the period of many years for most people.

Creating Wealth With Compound Interest

On the other hand, if we can multiply money - then everything changes. If we can earn a return on our money, grow our money, then earn a return on the growth in our money, and then earn a return on the return on the growth in our money - then we can reach a place where the earnings on our savings exceeds our new savings each year, and "our money is working for us", rather than "our working for our money".

The Homeowner Wealth Formula

This is the very heart of what has historically been the most reliable way for savers to build wealth over time, which is sometimes referred to as the "miracle" of compound interest.

As an example, let's say that an investor saved $1,000, and invested it at a 7% interest rate, which was about the historic average interest rate on 10 year U.S. Treasury obligations between 1962 and 2007.

At the end of one year, the investor would still have their starting savings, and 7% more money because of the interest payments. We take $1,000 multiply time 107% (1 plus "i", the interest rate), and we get $1,070 in ending savings.

Then in year two, we start not with $1,000, but $1,070. We multiply $1,070 times 107% again - and we get $1,145. We multiplied the multiplication, 107% times 107%, and we got an extra five dollars. The first year of interest earnings was $70, and the second year added another $75 on top of that. The source of the extra $5 was the interest earnings on the interest earnings, 7% interest earnings on the $70 in earnings from the first year.

In year three - we multiply the multiplication of the multiplication, which is 107% times 107% times 107%. We start with our $1,145, earn $80 in interest, and end up with $1,225 in savings. Our interest on interest earnings is now up to $10 per year, and we are also just starting to see a little bit of interest on interest on interest earnings.

What starts small builds over time into a compound interest wealth creation machine, that is driven by the full power of *exponential mathematics.*

With a 7% annual interest rate, the amount of money that we have doubles every ten years. If we start with $1,000, and then *we multiply it times 107% ten times in a row,* we get about $2,000 after ten years.

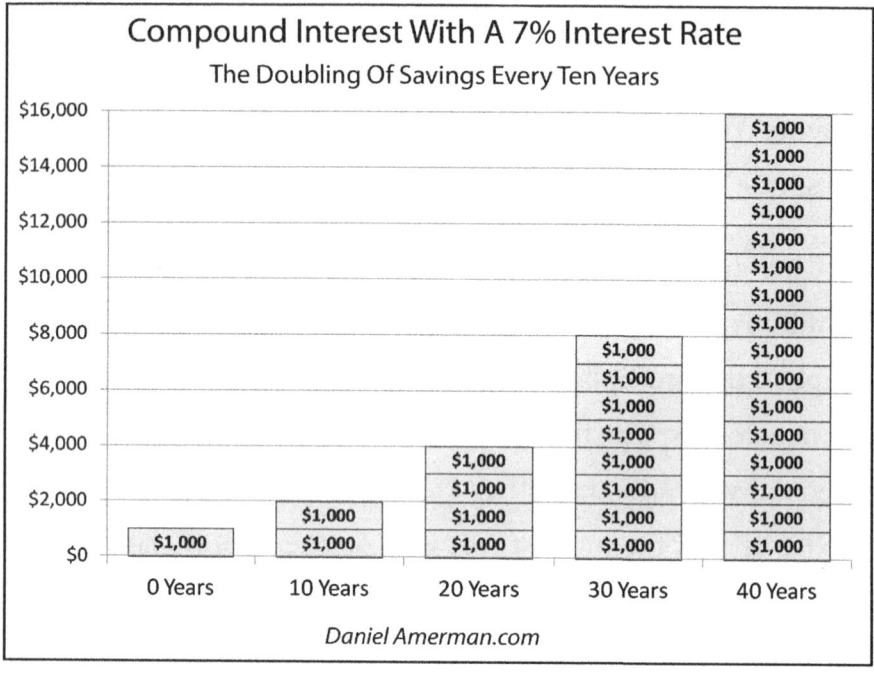

As shown in the compound interest graph above, one "block" of $1,000 doubles to become two blocks of $1,000 each over ten years. Those two blocks double again to become four blocks of $1,000 each over the next ten years, and then those four blocks double again to become eight blocks of $1,000 each over the following ten years. By the time we are forty years out, the doubling of the doubling of doubling of the doubling, means that $1,000 has become $16,000. (This is the same thing as multipling $1,000 times 107%, forty times in a row.)

By this time - we stopped working for that money a long time ago, we only saved the $1,000 one time. From that point forward, our money did the work on its own, eventually doubling again and again just given time, interest earnings, and the miracle of compound interest.

Compound interest is widely considered to be the most powerful and reliable source of wealth creation in human history. It we want to understand why the advice is so common when it comes to starting to save for retirement in our 20s or 30s - that formula and variants of it are the reason why. Give money time to work for us, let it multiply, and the multiplication of the multiplication (of the multiplication of the multiplication), can take a relatively small amount of initial savings and turn them into a wealth creation machine 10, 20 or 40 years later.

While most people don't realize this - compound interest also has a twin brother. It could even be called the evil twin brother, for it usually destroys wealth, relentlessly shredding financial security as well as the standards of living for entire nations.

Inflation Is Compound Interest

Like compound interest, inflation is a process of repeated multiplications over the years. In this case it is the annual multiplication of the amount of dollars it takes to buy things.

If it costs $1,000 to buy something, the price rises with inflation, and the annual rate of inflation is 7%, then we need to multiply $1,000 times 107% (1 plus "i", the rate of inflation), and it would cost $1,070 one year later. It takes 7% more dollars to buy the same product.

If there is a second year of 7% inflation, then we take the first year cost of $1,070 we multiply that times 107%, and the price by the end of the second year is $1,145. Of that, $70 is the first year of 7% inflation, $70 is the second year of 7% inflation, and the remaining $5 is - inflation compounding inflation.

The government does what it can to make sure that it costs more dollars to buy most things, on average, than it did the year before. This creates higher prices. The next year of inflation is then multiplied times those higher prices. And in the next year, those still higher prices are then multiplied again times the next year's rate of inflation.

If there is a third year of 7% inflation, then we start with the $1,145 price at the end of the second year, and multiply that times 107%, to find the new price after three years - which leads

The Homeowner Wealth Formula

to a new price of $1,225 after three years. The price rose $70 with the first year of inflation, $75 in the second year because both inflation and inflation on inflation, and then $80 in the third year, because of inflation and inflation compounding inflation.

If that process and those numbers sound familiar - they should. The formula for inflation is identical to that for compound interest. It is one plus "i", multiplied times itself (i.e. raised to the nth power) for the number of years. When calculating compound interest, then "i" is the interest rate, and when calculating inflation, then "i" is the rate of inflation.

When we are looking at the increase in the amount of savings with a 7% interest rate, then $1,000 becomes $1,070, and then $1,145, and then $1,225. When we look at the amount of money that it takes to buy something with a 7% inflation rate, then $1,000 becomes $1,070, and then $1,145, and then $1,225. The math and the compounding of the dollars are identical.

Inflation is indeed the evil twin of compound interest, and in general terms - it wreaks havoc with wealth instead of creating wealth. The longer the time that inflation has to run, then just like compound interest, the more powerful that it becomes, the greater the damage to the value of savings, and the more difficult that it becomes to protect oneself.

However, if someone owned an asset that had a very close relationship with inflation - like, say, a home - and the value of that asset were to climb with inflation, then *the numbers of dollars that it took to buy that asset would increase over the years with the full mathematical power of compound interest.*

To see how this works, let's use the round number example of a $100,000 home, with not a 7% interest rate, but a 7% rate of inflation. Each year, the price of buying most things rises, on average, by about 7%. Each year, the price of the home rises by 7%.

As with compound interest, after ten years with a 7% rate, there would be a doubling. Savings of $1,000 would become $2,000 over the ten years, the prices of cars and groceries would double - and the price of the home would double from $100,000 to $200,000.

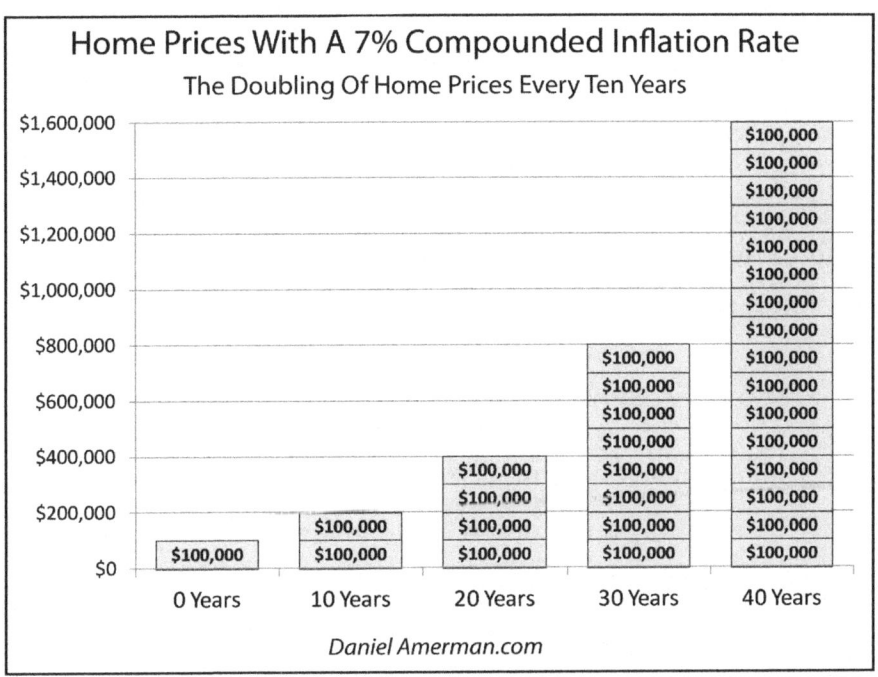

If the above graph looks familiar, then it should, but this time instead of the growth of savings we are looking at the impact of inflation on housing prices. The first $100,000 home price "block" doubles in ten years, becoming two $100,000 blocks. Those blocks double again to become four $100,000 blocks over the next ten years, and then double again to become eight $100,000 blocks over the following ten years. There would be another doubling over the next ten years, and after 40 years of 7% inflation, a home price that just kept up with inflation would have sixteen $100,000 blocks, meaning that the market value of the $100,000 home would be up to $1.6 million.

Compound interest is generally considered to be the most powerful and reliable creator of wealth in human history.

Simply owning a home with a mortgage has over the decades been the single most powerful and reliable creator of wealth for a normal middle class family in the United States (and other nations).

This is not a coincidence.

Underlying everything else, the core of the Homeowner Wealth Formula is an extremely reliable form of compound interest. Just home prices keeping up with inflation creates higher dollar prices in a formula that identical to that of the compound interest formula, with the only difference being substituting the rate of inflation for the interest rate.

This is the second level of the multiplication of wealth, the multiplication of the multiplication that occurs with inflation over multiple years, as home prices climb over time with the power of the compound interest formula.

This second level is the primary source of what creates most of the wealth, and as with other types of compound interest - the longer that it has to run, the longer we own the home, then the more powerful and reliable it becomes. Over the years, the doublings and the doublings of the doublings have represented an enormously powerful flow of wealth for those who were positioned to receive the benefits.

On a national average basis - inflation will take care of us when it comes to future home price gains over the long term. The government will do its absolute best to make sure that ever more dollars are required each year to pay for a given standard of living. Those dollars will steadily grow over time, as inflation builds on inflation in a one way process that has been highly reliable in the past.

The increasing dollars needed to buy almost anything will also be steadily, cumulatively building with the full power of the compound interest formula when it comes to the purchase price of the average home. Indeed, as covered in the previous chapter, there been a particularly tight relationship between cumulative increases in the consumer price index and cumulative increases in home prices.

On a very forgiving basis, inflation is likely to overwhelm everything else. Inflation makes it highly likely that the number of dollars required to buy our home in 10 or 20 years will be a great deal more than the dollars we originally paid for it, This means that our home equity will be far higher than what we started out with, all else being equal.

However, over shorter time periods, the role of inflation in creating more dollars for home prices can be less reliable. This is because the full power of the compound interest formula takes time to achieve, it is much less effective when it has less time to work. There has also been quite a bit a variation in annual rates of inflation, with very high rates in the 1970s and early 1980s, and much lower inflation rates in the 2000s and the 2010s. Soon a national average basis, what homeowners have experienced in practice over the short term has had a good deal of variability.

Average Homeowner Experiences With Inflation

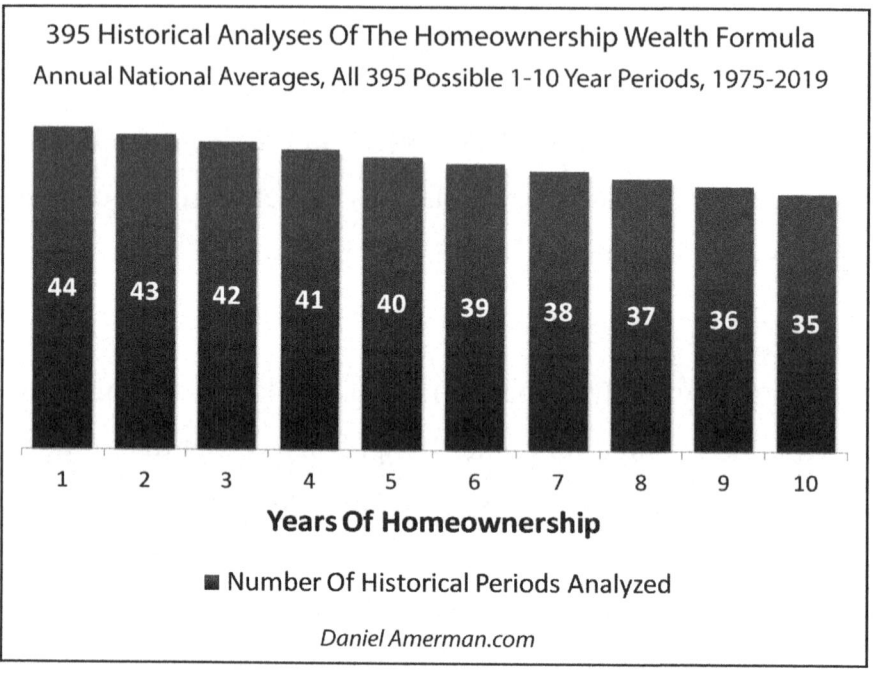

To get a better understanding of what homeowners have experienced in practice, and how much the average homeowner has benefited from inflation in shorter term periods, let's return to our analysis of 395 possible 1-10 year homeownership periods in the United States, between 1975 and 2019.

The Homeowner Wealth Formula

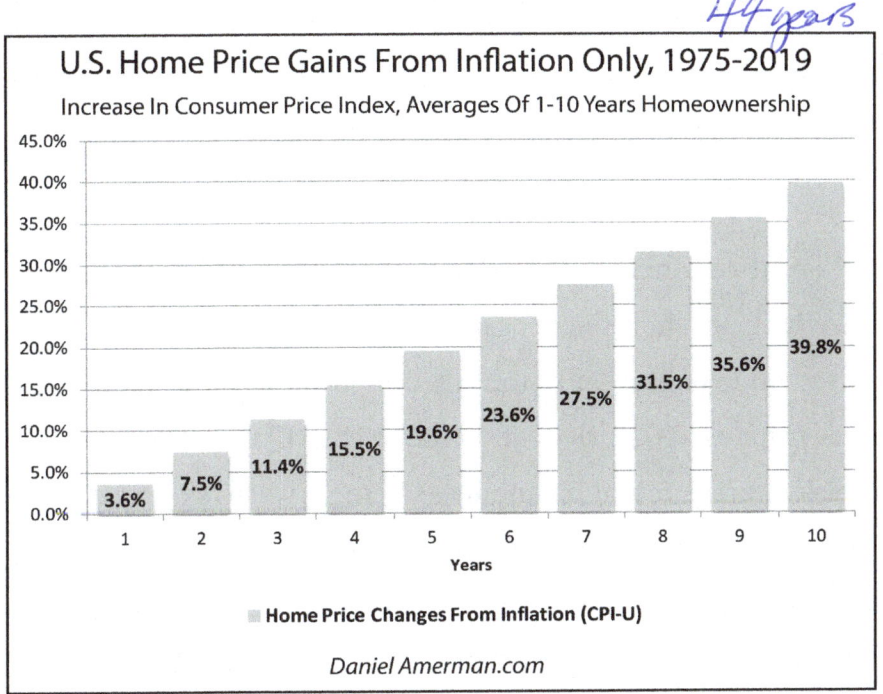

44 years

If we look at all 42 of the possible 3 year ownership periods between 1975-2019, including 1975-1978, 1992-1995, and 2016-2019, then the natural average result of inflation by itself for the average homeowner was to see the value of their home climb by 11.4% over the 3 years.

Looking at a round number starting home value of $200,000 (which is a little under the 2019 median home value of $225,000 for the United States), history shows that on average, just from inflation alone, the average home should gained about 11.4%. If our experience reflected historical averages, our home would be worth about $223,000 after 3 years, for a gain of $23,000.

That is $23,000 we would have if we had been making home mortgage payments, and $23,000 we wouldn't have if we had been making equally sized rental payments for those three years. Not bad.

(And yes, there are many other factors and expenses as well, which are the subject of Book #3 in this series, that is focused on expenses and monthly cash flow. For this first book, which is focused on prices and equity, we will treat homeowner expenses versus rental payments as being a wash, exactly equal to each other. When we do fully take those expenses into account, using the same 395 historical possible ownership periods, what we will find is a separate and quite powerful advantage to homeownership when it comes to monthly cash flow over the years, that can exceed the home equity increases that are the subject of Book #1 & Book #2.)

If we go out six years, and look at all 39 possible six year ownership periods, then just home prices keeping up with inflation by itself would have on average led to a 23.6% home price gain. Just that background force of the government steadily destroying the value of money, would have added another $47,000 to the value of our home. Almost an extra $50,000 of home equity, which is also not bad.

When we look national averages for all the 35 possible ten year ownership periods between 1975 and 2019 - then inflation by itself was enough to produce 39.8% more dollars being needed to buy a home over the 10 years. That almost 40% gain translates to about $80,000 in additional home value, and additional home equity.

For most people, that is starting to become some real money, that can be theirs as the result of alignment with a natural flow of wealth. Indeed, particularly for people in their 20s and 30s who are making rent versus buy decisions, that is the kind of difference that can carry forward for the rest of their lives when it comes to financial security.

This extraordinary natural flow of wealth happened, over and over and over again across the nation and the decades, and in many cases it changed the lives of the people involved, likely including some of the readers of this book as well as their parents. Now, most of the people involved may not have fully realized the degree of the relationship between inflation and home prices, and very few are likely to have graphed out the relationship between the consumer price index and the growing market price of their homes - but they didn't need to.

Just being in the position of homeownership was enough to benefit from the natural flow of wealth - on average. Because it was a natural flow - no deliberate intent or strategy was needed, it just happened in the natural course of things for all those millions of people, with what would become life changing increases in net worth and financial security as a result.

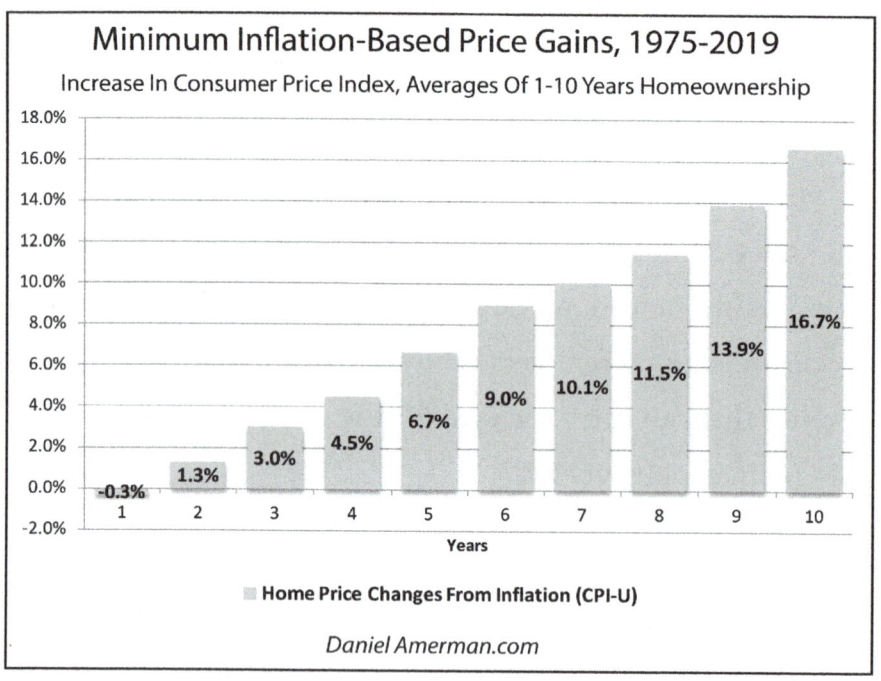

There is a range of outcomes, however, not everyone ended up with 40% higher home price due to inflation after ten years. If we look at the minimum amounts of inflation, then we find the exception, as shown in the 1 year homeownership column above. The consumer price index fell 0.3% between 2008 and 2009, and if we look at the relationship with inflation only, that would have been a $600 loss on a $200,000 home.

Now, actual losses were of course much higher during that time, as we will be covering when we focus on changes in inflation-adjusted home prices in Book #2, but if we isolate inflation by itself, there was only a single one year homeownership period where inflation failed to deliver positive price gains. The other 394 possibilities were all positive, and this wasn't an accident, nor was it random, but rather it is the result of the Federal Reserve using its extraordinary powers over the banking system and money itself to try to make sure that it took more dollars each year to buy the same things.

With three years of cumulative inflation to work with, the worst case out of all 42 three year homeownership periods was 3.0% (2013-2016), and that would have equated to about a $6,000 gain from inflation on a $200,000 home.

With six years of homeownership, the lowest gain from inflation out of all the possibilities was 9% (2011-2017), or an $18,000 gain on a $200,000 home.

When we look at ten years of the relentless, intentional, cumulative destruction of the purchasing power of the dollar, the minimum gain from inflation was 16.7% (2008-2018), which would be about a $33,000 gain on a $200,000 home.

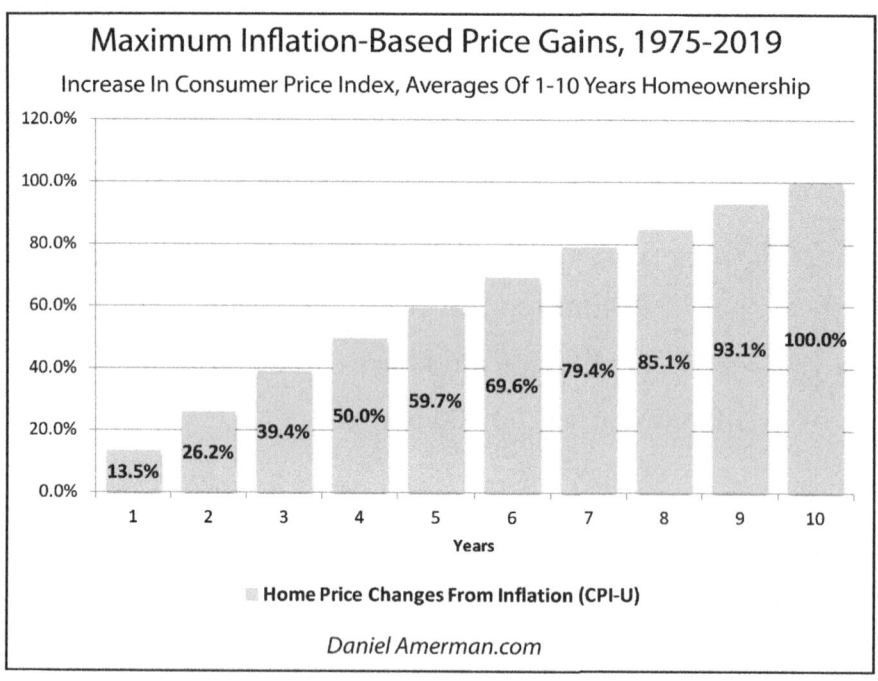

Each of those were the single worst historical results seen - the best results over the years are a quite different story. Looking at all the possible three year homeownership periods, the best result from inflation only was a 39.4% gain (1978-1981). For average homeowners over that period, if they had had a $200,000 home, that would have been about a $79,000 increase in home equity in just three years. Now, in practice, it would have been more likely to have been around a $43,000 home at the time, and a $17,000 gain, but the dollar was worth a lot more then, and the relative gain in home prices over the short term was equally dramatic.

When we look at the six year homeownership periods experienced by the nation, the maximum national average gains from inflation only were 69.6% (1976-1982). For an example $200,000 home (keeping comparability relative to modern home values, though home prices were lower at the time), what the nation experienced was an average $139,000 gain over six years.

Over ten years, the best result was a 100% gain in prices solely as a result of inflation - just like the round number 10 year example with home prices increasing with a 7% rate of inflation. Across the nation and on average, for homeowners who had bought in the year 1975, inflation would have doubled the value of their home by the year 1985, meaning they would have had an additional $200,000 in equity on what was originally a $200,000 home. That 100% gain was real, that is history, this is what happened in practice for millions of households (possibly including the parents of many of the people reading this book), and it changed many of their lives for decades thereafter.

Inflation & The Natural Flow Of Wealth

Now that we know the averages of the actual experiences for homeowners on a nationwide basis over the many years, and we also know the ranges of what people have experienced in practice, that gives us much better information to work with in understanding the portion of the homeowner wealth formula that is based on inflation, and the historical relationship between inflation and home prices.

For the 42 three year homeownership periods between 1975 and 2019, the average nationwide gain from inflation only would have been 11.4%. The minimum that was actually experienced was 3.0%, and the maximum gain for homeowners was 39.4%.

Using a $200,000 home as an example to illustrate the percentages, then on average, homeowners gained about $23,000 in home equity from inflation only in three years. The worst result out of all 42 possibilities was to gain about $6,000, and the best result of all 42 possibilities was to gain about $79,000 in home equity just from inflation.

As discussed in Chapter 1, for something to be a "natural flow of wealth", the completely average result should be to do well - no special skill, timing or luck required. Just choosing to be in that position should, by itself, deliver desirable results on average. There should be the ability to do much better if one is particularly skillful or particularly lucky. The natural flow should also be forgiving, so that if someone in practice turns out to be unskillful or unlucky, there is a good chance of coming out ahead anyway.

When we apply those tests to inflation only over three years - all are met. A $23,000 gain in three years is a quite attractive average result (particularly if we compare it not to the total home price but the original down payment, as we will do in later chapters). If we do really well, the upside is to make more than three times as much money than the average. If we happen to experience the very worst, well, on a national average basis we would still be up by $6,000, which while not thrilling, isn't that bad either.

When we move our test to the six year homeownership periods that were actually experienced by the nation, then the inflation component by itself continues to deliver. Average gains were 23.6%, the minimum experienced was 9.0%, and the maximum national average gains experienced were 69.6%.

On a $200,000 home, the $47,000 average gain is very attractive, the minimum $18,000 gain is not bad at all for the worst case experienced, and the possible $139,000 gain to the upside is downright stunning for just six years.

It is also worth comparing the minimums between the three and six year periods, because there is some good information value there. The 3% gain over three years needs to be seen for what it is - a failure on the part of the Federal Reserve to achieve its goals. The Fed intended to destroy roughly about 2% of the value of the dollar each year over the three years, it only succeeded in destroying 1% per year, and that was the worst failure on the part of the Fed to reach its minimum inflation targets out of all of the 42 three year periods studied.

Inflation is a deliberate, relentless, cumulative, one way destruction of the value of the dollar. This means that it is a deliberate, relentless, cumulative, one way process that unleashes the power of the compound interest formula in making sure ever more dollars are required to buy things - single family homes in this case. Using its extraordinary powers with six years to work with, on a cumulative basis - the Federal Reserve did significantly better. A 9% gain over six years could be called roughly a 1.5% annual rate of inflation (that isn't the actual compounding math, but close enough for now), so it came much closer to meeting its goal.

The longer we are in the home, the more time the Fed has to work with in trying to meet its goals, the more reliable it becomes in meeting those goals of requiring ever more money to buy everything, and the more forgiving the inflation component of homeownership becomes.

When we move our "natural flow of wealth" test to ten year homeownership periods, then the average result of an almost $80,000 increase in equity for an example $200,000 home is starting to become a truly life changing result for an average person. Just from inflation alone, and from being in the position of being a homeowner instead of a renter, that is tremendous increase in home equity.

Our minimum result is indeed that much more forgiving with the passage of four more years, and is now up to $33,000, which for the worst single ten year result experienced in practice and on average by the nation on a percentage basis over the 44 years analyzed - is not bad at all.

The best result experienced by the nation as a whole was that of inflation and the power of the compound interest being enough to double the home prices, and double the example home from $200,000 from $400,000. This is an extraordinary average result for a nation as a whole, and it also serves as the counterpoint to the minimum results when it comes to the two sources of inflation that the nation has in fact experienced.

The minimum inflation results were the entirely intentional results of a Federal Reserve determined to use its extraordinary powers to force down the purchasing power of the dollar in a relentless and cumulative process.

However, the great majority of the doubling of the consumer price index between 1975 and 1985 - and the halving of the purchasing power of the dollar - was a complete accident. Sometimes central banks screw up, and sometimes nations face bursts of inflation from sources they have little control over. In this case, the Fed completely lost control over inflation, and had a very difficult time reestablishing control.

So the Fed maintaining control sets the minimum, that still results in ever more equity for homeowners in a steady, cumulative, one way process. And when the Fed completely loses control - even more equity can flow to homeowners, on a much faster basis.

Those two sources in combination are very good to keep in mind for the 2020s, as the dominance of the Federal Reserve over the financial system and the economy reaches all new levels, even as the risks of a national debt soaring out of control that is effectively being funded by the Federal Reserve just creating the money to do so, pose ever greater threats to the long term purchasing power of the dollar.

Chapter 4

Turning Inflation Into Wealth With A Home & Mortgage

The next step in assembling the Homeowner Wealth Formula is to include a mortgage. Not everyone uses a mortgage, however, the majority of people do so when buying a home - particularly when buying their first home. When a mortgage is added, then one of the most powerful wealth flows in history is unleashed over the years that follow.

Indeed for many tens of millions of households over the decades, this natural flow of wealth has been the single best investment they have ever made. This natural flow has in practice become the number one source of financial security for many of them, creating more net worth than any other decisions they made - even if they didn't understand any of this in advance, or thought about this being the natural result of their using a mortgage to become a homeowner.

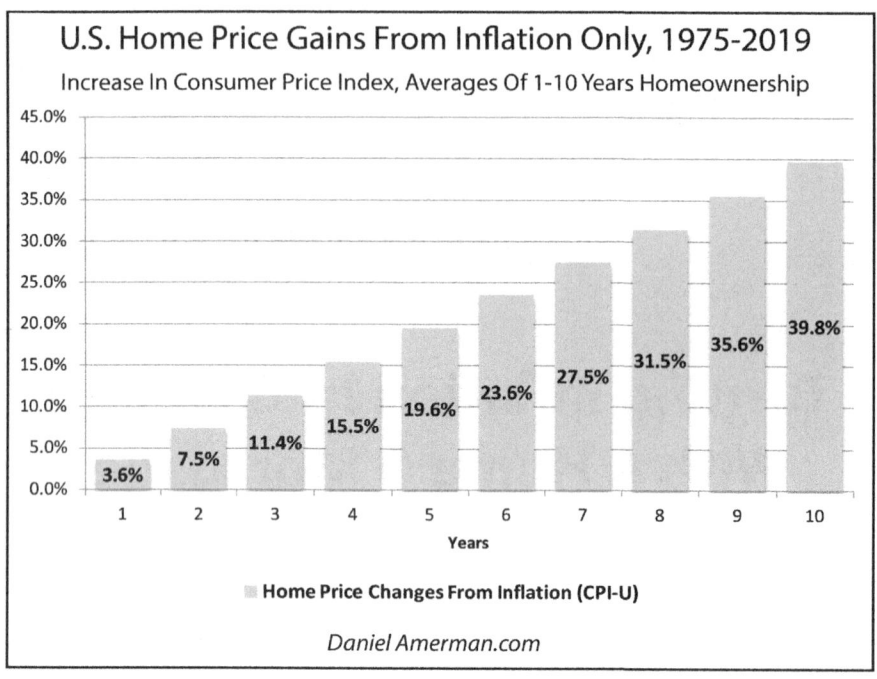

As developed in previous chapters, there has been a very close historical linkage between inflation as measured by increases in the Consumer Price Index and increases in national average home prices. If we take the simplifying step of looking at national average home prices that would come from inflation only, then we get the graph above. If their homes had just exactly kept up with inflation, then on average and over the decades, the average homeowner would have seen the value of their property rise by almost 20% over the first five years, and by almost 40% over their first ten years in their home. Not bad at all.

The Homeowner Wealth Formula

The graph below puts a flat line under home equity, and shows what happens with an 80% LTV (loan-to-value) mortgage. When the home was purchased, the homeowner put up 20%, and the mortgage lender put up 80%, as can be seen on the left in year 0.

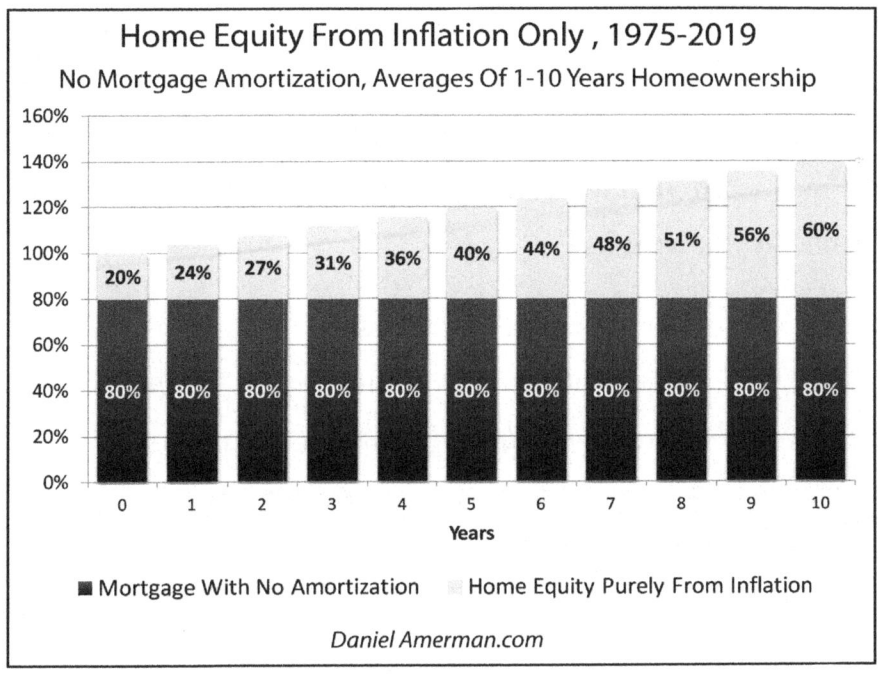

Now, mortgages amortize, meaning a portion of each month's payment goes to paying down what is owed on the loan. This is very important - but when it comes to sources of homeowner wealth it isn't generally as important as the overall relationship between mortgages, inflation and home prices, particularly in the early years of home ownership. Amortization is also a bit of a complication. So for simplicity and clear communication in these next several chapters we won't include amortization. When we do add amortization starting in Chapter 8, it will be a separate factor that will lead to further increases in homeowner equity, while further reducing homeowner risks.

In combination then, we are taking two simplifying steps in order to isolate and focus on a key component of the Homeowner Wealth Formula. We are using just the historical inflation component of home price increases, and we are also using a flat debt that doesn't pay down. Those two forces in combination are however enough to unleash an extraordinarily powerful and reliable flow of wealth.

The source of this extraordinary flow of wealth is that while the mortgage lender puts up 80% of the money - *all increases in home value that are created by inflation and the compound interest formula go to the benefit of the homeowner, and none go to the benefit of the mortgage lender.*

Over the decades, when inflation by itself caused the number of dollars needed to buy most things to go up by 4% in the first year - including single family homes - all of that went to the homeowners and none to the lenders. So, with no amortization (yet), and relative to the original purchase price of the home, the homeowner is up from 20% to 24% in one year - while the lender stays flat at 80%.

The homeowner reaping all the benefits from just inflation by itself, while the lender does not participate - has historically swiftly built net worth for homeowners.

An Unequal Partnership

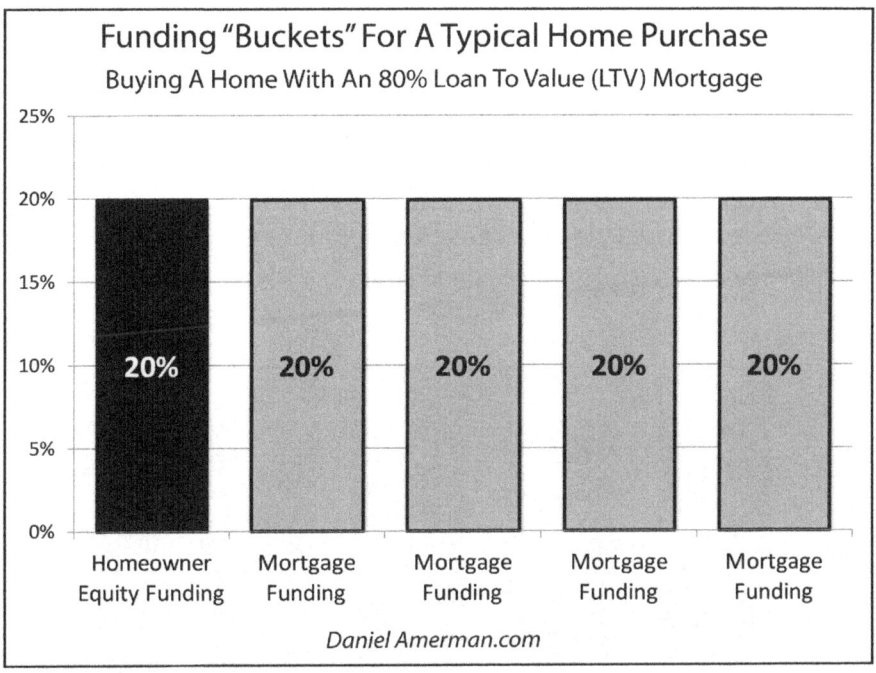

If the home buyer takes out an 80% loan to value mortgage to buy their home, then a useful way of looking at this is to break up the financing of the home purchase into five different "buckets" of 20% each. The mortgage lender contributes four of the 20% buckets, the home buyer puts up one 20% bucket.

If we look at this in dollar terms for a $200,000 house then the homebuyer would put up $40,000 in equity, and the mortgage lender would put up $160,000 - which is equal to four buckets of $40,000 each.

Now, leaving everything else aside, and just looking at inflation with no mortgage amortization, let's say that inflation increases the average price of buying anything and everything by 20% - and this includes our home. If we look at all 40 of the possible five year homeownership periods between 1975 and 2019, then the average increase in the Consumer Price Index over five years was indeed equal to about 20% (rounded).

Next, let's move the scale to 100%, because we are looking at percentage gains on the initial equity only. The homeowner puts in $40,000 which is 100% of their equity contribution at closing, and the mortgage lender puts in four more equal amounts, each of which also equals 100% of the equity contribution.

If inflation increases the prices of everything over five years - which on a national average basis it did over all of the five year periods between 1975 and 2019 - and the home merely exactly kept up with inflation, then it should increase in price by 20%. The portion of the home purchased with homebuyer equity would rise by 20% - and each of the four contributions by the mortgage lender would also rise by 20%.

Assuming a $200,000 home, our 20% equity "bucket" would therefore increase in price by 20%, which would be $8,000. We would own that, free and clear.

Now, if the homeowner and the mortgage lender had an equal, equity partnership, where the mortgage lender owned 80% of the house because they had put up 80% of the money, then they would get the 20% inflation gains for each of their four buckets.

However, because we have an unequal partnership with the mortgage lender, they don't get any of the gains. So, we don't just get the 20% gains on our own bucket, but we get the entire 20% inflation-based price gains from all four of the lender's buckets.

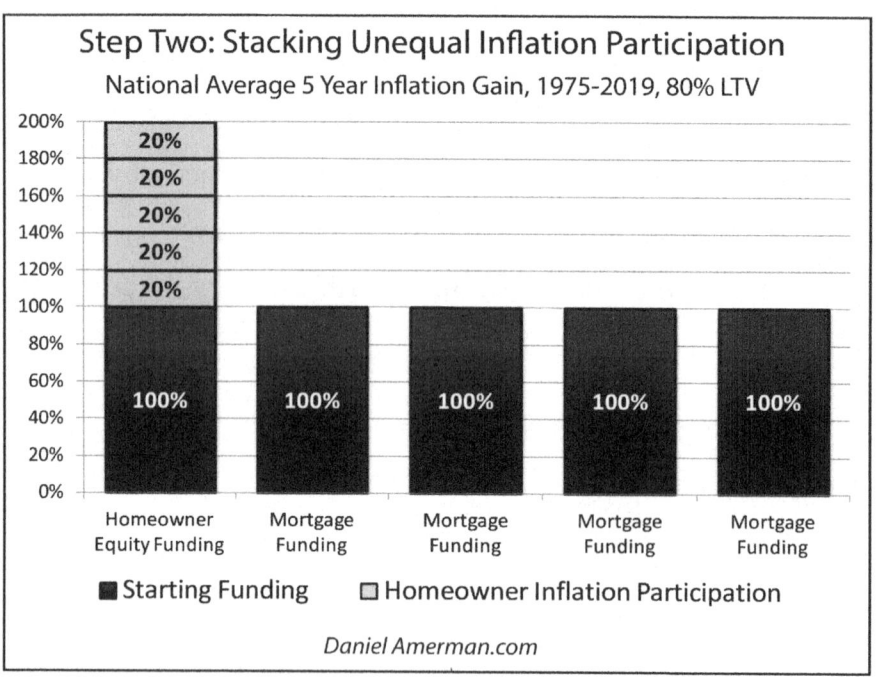

When we start with our 20% gain, and then stack all four of the 20% gains associated with the share of the home purchased with money from the mortgage lender - but that we don't share with the lender - then we have five individual 20% gains from inflation, all stacked on top of each other.

That is a 100% gain, which means we would have doubled our money, in terms of equity - in only five years, and not from market speculation, but just from a historically normal rate of inflation.

To put it in dollar terms for a $200,000 home, all five of the $40,000 buckets would have gone up 20% each, which would have been an $8,000 price increase for each bucket. We would get all five of those $8,000 gains, which is $40,000 - and again, we doubled our original $40,000 investment, from historically normal inflation only, and in just five years, while the lender's share is $0. (Banks have many ways of taking advantage of ordinary people, this is one of the few ways for consumers to take advantage of the banks.)

Another way of looking at it, is to just say that a $200,000 home was purchased with a $160,000 mortgage, and that it increased in price by 20% over five years purely as a result of just keeping even with normal inflation. That means it would be a $240,000 house, the (non-amortizing) mortgage would still be $160,000, there would now be $80,000 in equity, and that would be double the original equity investment.

Whether we look at in percentages or dollars, there are two crucial numbers here, a quintupling and a doubling. When we put up only 20% of the money to buy an asset that goes up with inflation - but we get 100% of the inflation-based price gains, which is five times what we funded - then we multiply the rate of inflation times five, meaning *we quintuple the rate of inflation.*

This quintupling of 20% inflation creates a doubling of home equity and means that we have *turned inflation into wealth.*

This is the third level of the multiplication of wealth, the multiplication and five high stacking that occurs with compounded inflation gains relative to home equity when a home is purchased with a mortgage.

How this worked out historically for the homeowners of the nation as a whole over the decades, assuming an 80% LTV mortgage, is that inflation by itself on average doubled their equity in just their first five years of owning a home. That remarkable result is not the exception but the average experience of many tens of millions of homeowners, and it occurred whether or not they had any idea of the mathematics of where that very pleasant increase in net worth was coming from.

An Unequal Partnership Over Ten Years

The longer the time period, then the greater the relentless, deliberate and cumulative destruction of the purchasing power of money, the greater the power of the compound interest formula, and the more thorough the job that inflation does of destroying the value of savings. This also means that the longer the time period - the more dollars it takes to buy an average home (all else being equal). When we consider what history shows us about homes with mortgages, the longer the time period, then the more powerful the ability to turn a negative into a positive, and to create wealth from inflation.

When we move out ten years, and we look at all 35 of the ten year time periods between 1975 and 2019, then we find that on average it took about 40% more dollars to buy anything and everything by the end of the ten years.

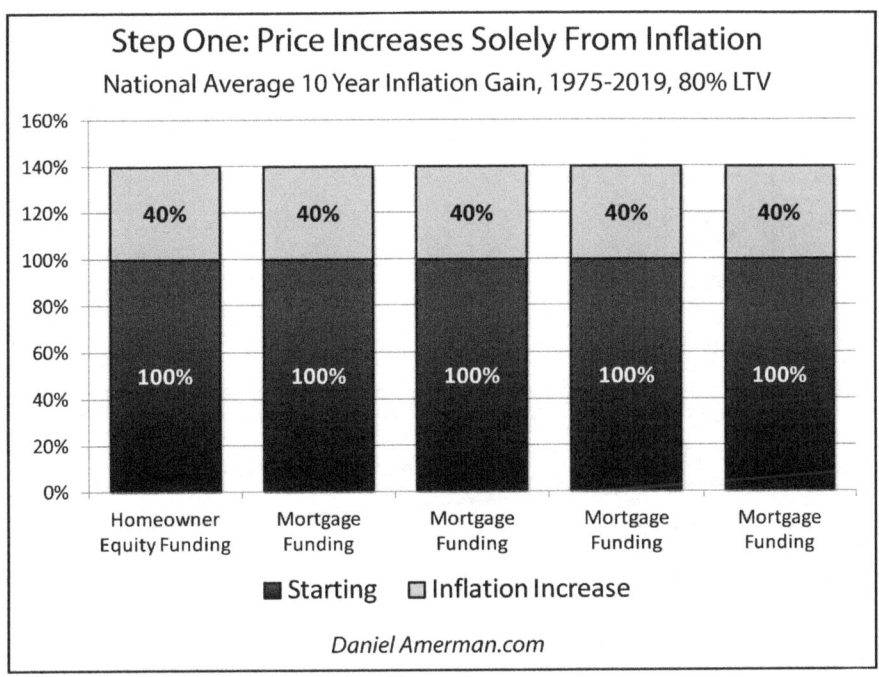

When we look at the five buckets - we are now up to a 40% gain on our original equity down payment. Much more importantly - all four of the mortgage lender buckets are also up by 40%, just as the normal result of ten years of historically average inflation.

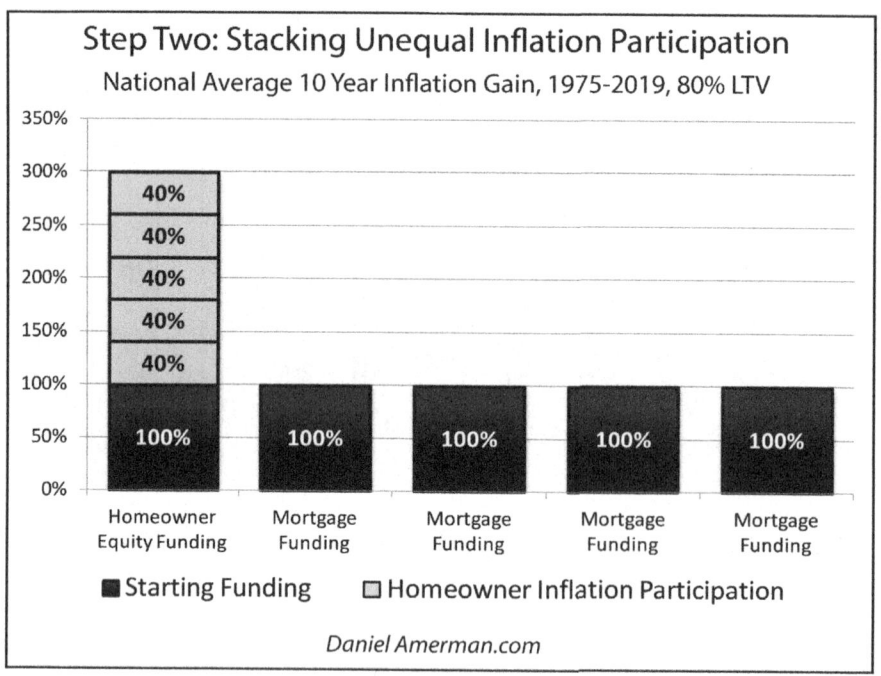

The same principles apply for ten years as for five years - the numbers just get bigger. The homeowner who put up 20% of the purchase price still gets 100% of the inflation price gains, while the lender gets 0% under the contractual terms of the unequal partnership.

Stacking all five of the 40% inflation price gains on top of each other means that the homeowner earns a 200% gain relative to their original investment. *The national average outcome for homeowners (with an 80% LTV mortgage) has been to turn inflation into wealth and to triple their equity in their first ten years of homeownership* - just from that inflation alone, nothing else. In other words, the national average outcome over the decades has been to turn inflation into wealth.

Relative to the original buckets, the homeowner would gain 40% or $16,000 on their $40,000 equity investment. The other four buckets of $40,000 would also go up by $16,000 each, just as the natural result of inflation over time. Multiplying the $16,000 gain times five, that is an $80,000 inflation-based gain, which is equal to 200% of the original homeowner investment, and means that the equity has tripled from $40,000 up to $120,000.

All of that gain of would go to the homeowner who put up $40,000 initially, and none would go to the mortgage lender who put up $160,000 initially. That is a tripling in ten years - and it based on taking a 40% increase in price levels, reversing the destructive impact of inflation through using a home with a mortgage, and turning that inflation into a 200% increase in wealth.

Tripling equity in ten years is an amazing result. But that is our actual average history, and tens of millions of households have experienced this in practice over their first ten years of home ownership, whether they first bought in the 1970s, 1980s, 1990s or 2000s. This natural flow of wealth was the result of just being in the position of owning a home that was bought with the help of a mortgage.

Those many millions of homeowners may not have known why their home equity rose by that amount. And of course, the specifics would have varied greatly, depending on the years, the metro areas, the neighborhoods, and the individual homes. But on average, there were huge gains in equity over all those years for people who used mortgages to buy homes, as the very direct result of the relationship between inflation and debt explored in these chapters.

The Historical Experience For All Ten Years

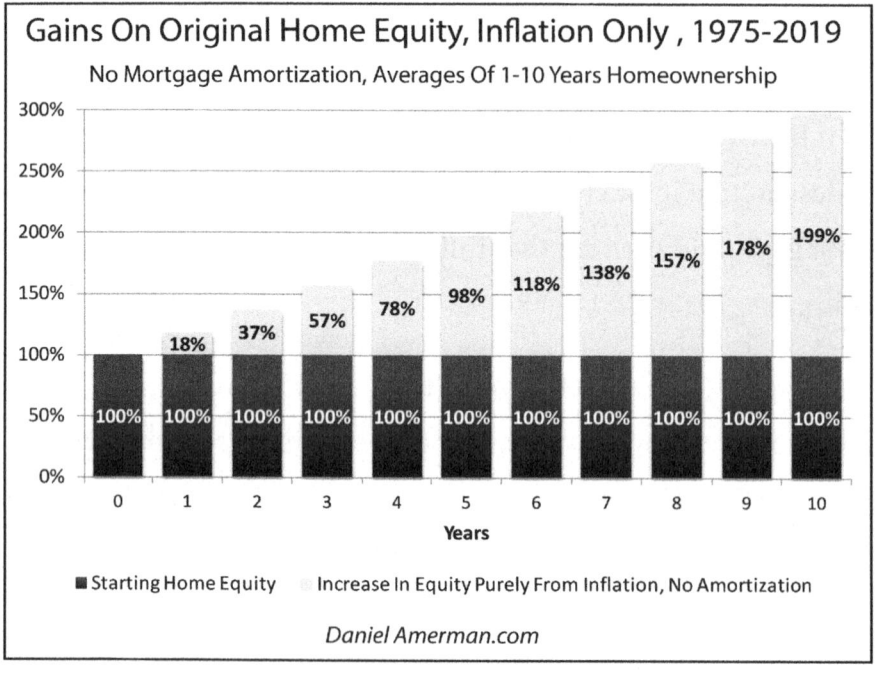

The graph above takes all 395 of the one to ten year possible homeownership periods between 1975 and 2019, and shows the remarkable results when we combine just the historical inflation in each time period, and then look at how the five buckets would have multiplied the starting home equity with an 80% LTV mortgage.

An 18% equity gain in one year is the average result for the nation.

Over a 50% increase in the first three years - was the normal outcome over all those years.

We've already reviewed the five and ten year results, which are a doubling and a tripling (although calculated with another decimal place of precision for the particular graph above).

The completely typical experience was a 150% increase in home equity in eight years.

Indeed, for readers who own homes and have done so for years or decades, perhaps several homes over the years - what you see above is quite likely a description of what happened to you personally, or one of the most powerful background forces that impacted what happened to you personally and the equity you had in your home or homes over the years.

Now, some might say that this doesn't matter - because while there is a very strong relationship between home prices and inflation, they are not the same thing. There is some truth to that. The historical facts are that while inflation by itself with a non-amortizing mortgage is enough to triple equity in ten years - when we use actual national average home price histories with the corresponding national average mortgage amortizations over those years, then the average was for homeowners with a mortgage (80% LTV) to more than quadruple their equity over their first ten years of homeownership.

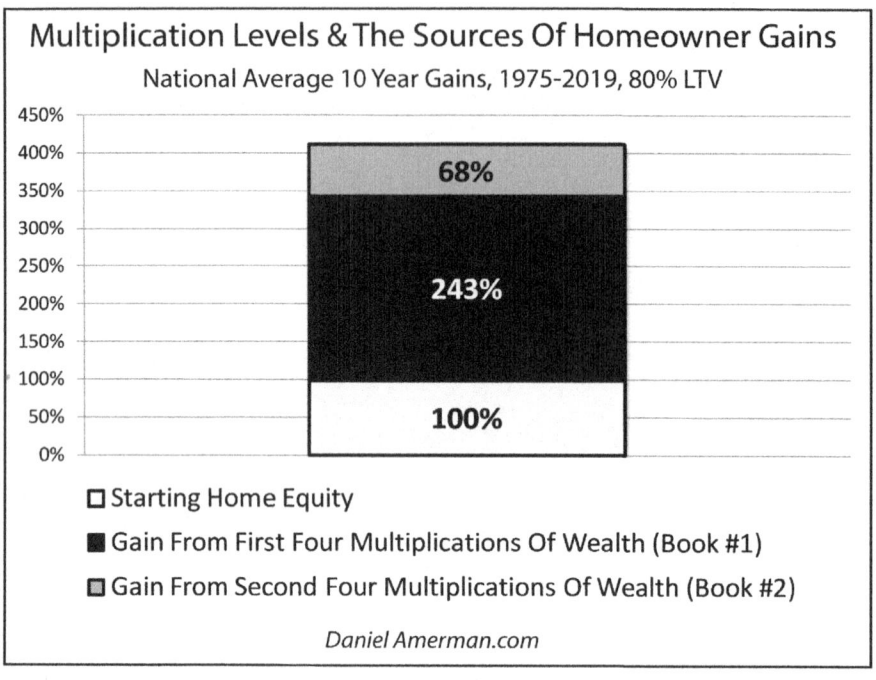

So, inflation and a non-amortizing mortgage are not all of the Homeownership Wealth Formula - but, as explored in this chapter and the immediately following chapters, they are most of it. When we take all the components of the Homeownership Wealth Formula into account and all eight levels of the multiplication of wealth, as will be assembled step by step over the rest of this book and Book #2, then we have an average of 4.1X the equity after 10 years. Of that increase, about 3X the equity can be explained solely by what we just reviewed, the combined result of the first three levels of the multiplication of wealth.

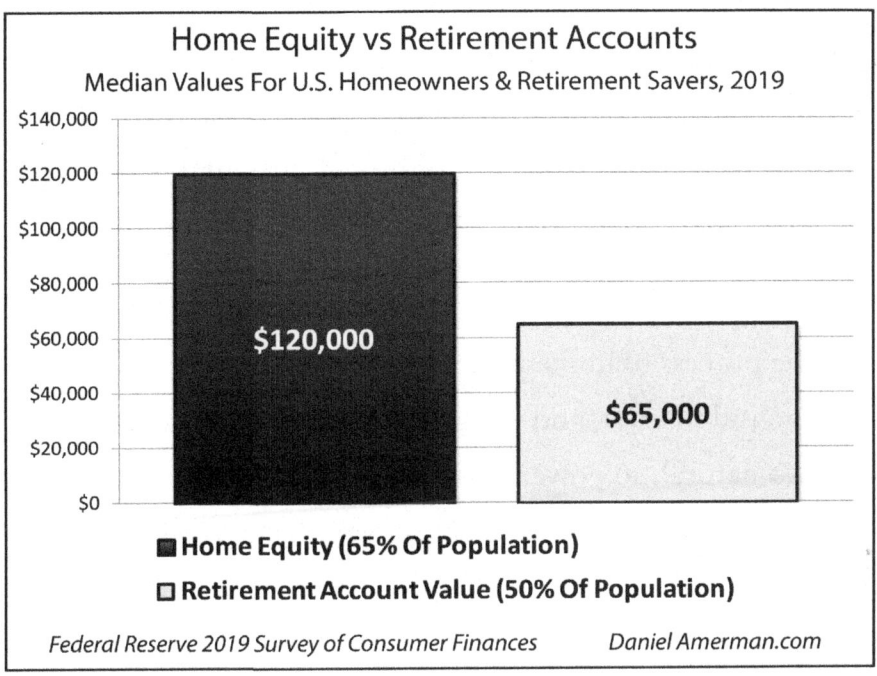

When we understand how homeownership with a mortgage takes compounded inflation and stacks it five high - then the above graph of national median home equity versus median retirement account balances can make a lot more sense. Generally speaking, people don't set out to build net worth by buying a home, they set out to build net worth by buying investments such as stocks and bonds, often while using the tax advantages of holding those assets in a retirement account.

Retirement accounts are a very focused and deliberate process of intentionally building net worth over the long term. They are indeed a wonderful way of building financial security and wealth - but retirement accounts do take time and discipline.

Meanwhile, the average lived experience is that while people intensely focus on deliberately building their net worth through their retirement account investments, close to twice the net worth for homeowners is coming in unobserved through the back door on a more or less accidental basis, in the form of increases in home equity.

The process of home prices growing with the same formula as compound interest, and then stacking those inflation gains five high is so natural, so powerful, and so reliable over time, that for the average person in practice it has overwhelmed the benefits of intentionally building net worth via retirement accounts.

Playing Off An Artificial Intervention Against An Unequal Partnership To Create A Natural Flow Of Wealth

There are those who would say that what we have just reviewed is a simple example of leverage. Leverage is a popular way to multiply profits - or multiply losses - by using borrowed money to finance at least part of an investment.

There is of course a long and close relationship between real estate investment and leverage. The use of leverage has created many real estate millionaires and multimillionaires over the years - and it has also bankrupted many real estate investors as well.

However, not all leverage is created equal. And indeed, the results associated with long term homeownership are not at all what would be expected for high risk, leveraged investments. The gains are very large over time, as would be expected with leverage, but the downside is not nearly as large as one would expect. Indeed, the great majority of results are highly positive, and the negatives are far fewer - particularly when we move beyond short term ownership.

In the next chapter, we will focus on the sources of why the positive results are overwhelmingly more common and larger than the negative results.

Why An 80% LTV Mortgage?

The natural flow of wealth depends on all three components: the home, inflation and the mortgage. Without inflation (at this stage), there is no increase in home prices. Without the mortgage, we just have an asset that keeps up with inflation. That is very nice and a strong positive - a lot of assets including money itself do not keep up. But with no mortgage, there is no turning inflation into wealth, and there is no creating new wealth in the form of home equity at a rate that far exceeds the destruction of the purchasing power of money.

Now, if someone owns a home free and clear, then they have no mortgage payment, which can be a very attractive position when it comes to monthly cash flow. But the base assumption for this Book #1, is that that is not the case, someone needs a residence for themselves and their family, and they don't have the money to pay cash. For simplicity, we are treating rent payments and mortgage payments as being equal, so they more or less cancel out and we are looking at the gains on the money that was invested to make the down payment, or starting home equity. (Again, as covered in Book #3, mortgage payments do not actually cancel out when compared to rent payments over time, but become a second and equally powerful source of advantage.)

Over the next few years and the next decade - are there potentially life changing differences between renters and home owners? Well, what history shows us is that there are indeed life changing differences, and that a side effect of buying a home with a mortgage is to unlock an extraordinarily powerful flow of wealth that can persist and build for many years, but which renters simply don't have access to. (The flow of wealth is still there, it just goes to the property owner instead of the renter, and by making their rental payments the renter makes the landlord's mortgage payments which unlocks the flow of wealth for the landlord.)

The amount of debt relative to the purchase price of the home is very important. With a 50% loan to value (LTV), a

$200,000 home would be bought with a $100,000 mortgage, and $100,000 in initial equity. A historic average inflation-based increase in value of 40% over ten years would lead to a home value of $280,000, of which $180,000 would be equity. This would be an 80% increase in equity with a 50% LTV mortgage, instead of the 200% increase that we saw with the 80% LTV mortgage. That is still very good, and still turns inflation into wealth, just at a substantially lower rate.

On the other hand, with a 90% LTV mortgage, the mortgage lender would put up $180,000, and the homeowner would put up only $20,000 in initial equity. So a home value of $280,000 would create $100,000 in equity, which is a 400% increase in equity relative to the starting $20,000, instead of the 200% increase seen with a 80% LTV mortgage.

There is a very strong risk/return relationship when it comes to the amount of mortgage borrowing and turning inflation into wealth.

For me, this is fascinating stuff, and working through risk/return relationships and finding optimal positions has been a good part of my career. Risk/return relationships were key to my investment analysis books for mortgage securities that were published in the 1990s, and they are crucial for my asset/liability management workshops and video course for real estate investors.

However, including them in this book for the general public, and working through every aspect of the formula with a range of

LTV ratios while analyzing the implications for each ratio - would exponentially increase the complexity of this book. Increasing the complexity to something closer to professional grade is good for investing but is not needed for simple homeownership and would unnecessarily screen out large numbers of normal people - so this book avoids excess complexity by sticking to one LTV, that of an assumed 80% loan to value mortgage, with a fixed interest rate and a 30 year term.

There are three reasons for selecting an 80% LTV in this exploration of national historic averages.

1) Eighty percent loan to value mortgages are very common. The reason for this is that most 30 year mortgage loans are "conventional", meaning they conform to Fannie Mae and Freddie Mac underwriting guidelines, and those guidelines require mortgage insurance if a mortgage has over an 80% LTV. This can be expensive for homeowners. It can also take a higher credit score to qualify for an LTV of over 80%. So, for reasons of qualifying for the mortgage, and avoiding adding a mortgage insurance premium to each mortgage payment, many borrowers do not go above 80% if they can avoid it.

2) Even in the worst years after the collapse of the real estate bubble and in the recession and financial crisis of 2008 - on a national average annual basis, there were no underwater mortgages with an 80% LTV, meaning that home values went below the mortgage amount and created negative home equity.

Oh, it was very close, right on the edge, and 80% LTVs did in the very worst years create negative equity on average in some metro areas, but not on a national average basis.

3) Even if we look at the absolute worst cases, the very worst years, there are no instances of losing equity on a national average basis for people who are in their homes for at least nine years. Indeed, as we will develop in Book #2, the worst case absolute minimum gain in equity on a national average basis for people with an original 80% LTV who were in their home for ten years was a 60%+ equity gain. Looking at all 35 of the possible ten year homeownership periods between 1975 and 2019, to have the single worst result be to be up over 60% isn't bad.

Chapter 5

The Long History Of Using Inflation & Homes To Multiply Wealth

The term leverage is usually associated with taking high risk positions for maximum gains. It could be stock market speculation with money borrowed on margin, or it could be real estate speculation, trying to use as much borrowed money as possible to buy a property and flip it for a profit a few months later. There are strong similarities with going to a casino, or buying lottery tickets. Sometimes you win in a big way - and sometimes you lose, in a possibly catastrophic way.

If this were what was happening with homeownership, and every time someone had bought a home thinking they were just buying a three bedroom place to live in a nice neighborhood - but what they were actually doing was entering a casino and rolling the dice with some unintended high risk leveraged speculation -

then the history of homeownership in the U.S. should be littered with accidental victims.

All through the 1970s, 1980s, 1990s, 2000s and 2010s - there should have been a non-stop stream of surprised homeowners, thinking they were just buying a home, but instead losing everything they had when they found out they had accidentally been making leveraged bets in a high stakes casino, and had been unlucky.

However, as previously reviewed, that is not at all how homeownership has actually worked over the decades in the United States. Yes, based on national averages, becoming a homeowner has been an amazingly good investment in terms of increases in the equity invested - which would be compatible with a leveraged investment. However, there has also (over the long term) been a great deal of consistency, homeowners almost always come out ahead - and that would not seem to be compatible with a leveraged investment, there should be frequent major losses along the way.

As we will review in this chapter, the reason is that on average - homeowners are not speculating in a securities market or on some random outcome. They are instead aligning themselves with something that is not chance but is entirely deliberate, which is the stated policies of the United States government (in the form of the Federal Reserve).

A Stated Policy Of Destroying The Value Of Money

As we reviewed in Chapters 2 & 3 in particular, the stated policy of the Federal Reserve is to try to destroy a low to moderate bit of the value of money every year, without exception. Oh, they don't quite phrase it that way, but the explicitly stated policy is that their goal is usually that they want it take around 2% more dollars each year to pay for a normal standard of living, when compared to the year before.

This by itself puts inflation in a very different category than playing in a casino, or borrowing to play the markets. Inflation is a matter of government policy. Indeed the government policy over the years could be said to set the floor, with inflation sometimes climbing well above it.

So, homeowners aren't really guessing about what is going to happen - particularly over the long term - as much as they are aligning themselves with a government policy. That then raises the question of just how much money homeowners should expect to make solely from that government policy, assuming that the government (on average) exactly meets its inflation target over the coming years?

If we take a round number target of a 2% rate of inflation, and run it out for ten years using the compound interest formula, then the 2% builds on the 2%, which builds on the 2%, and the total over ten years is a 22% increase in the number of dollars it takes to buy things - including homes.

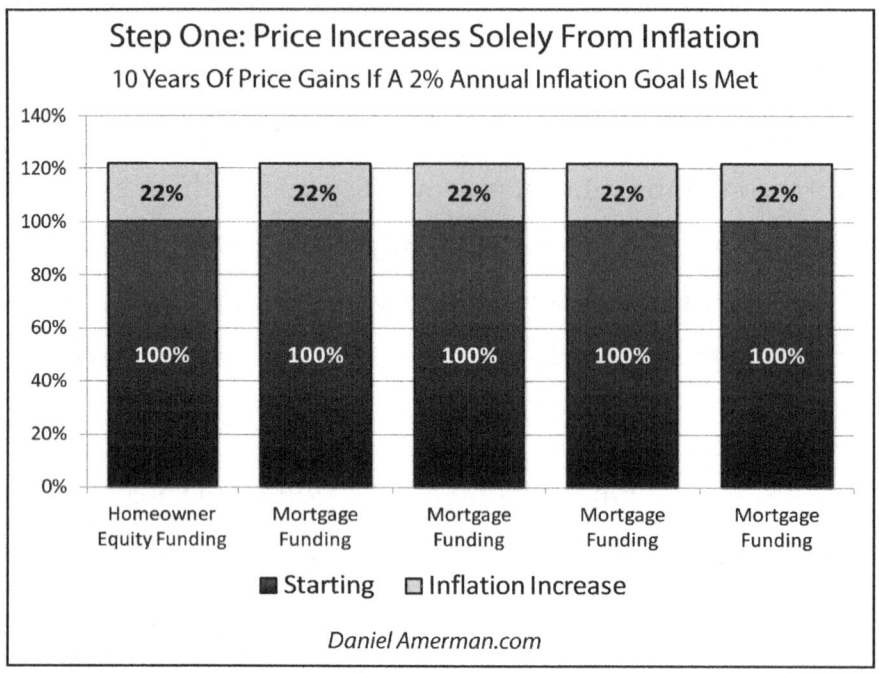

So, we have a 22% gain on our original equity investment. There are also 22% gains on each of the other four buckets, assuming an 80% LTV mortgage. Because of the unequal partnership, the mortgage lender receives none of the inflation gains, and we get all of them.

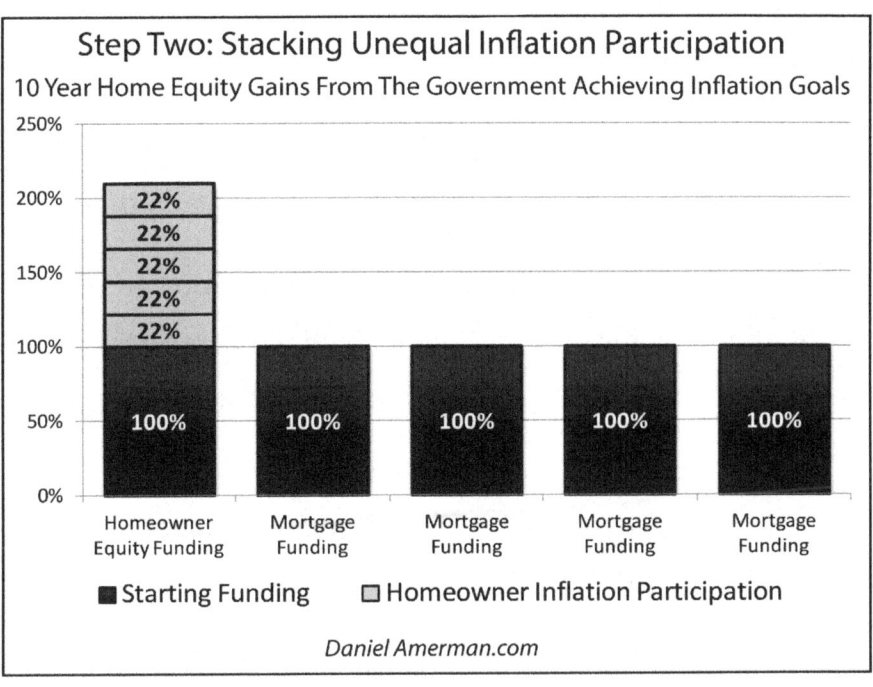

When we stack up the 22% gains, then we are multiplying times five, and the total gain for the homeowner is 110%. This means that if the government were to meet its stated policy goal of a 2% annual rate of inflation, and if homes exactly kept up with that rate of inflation - then the average homeowner would see their equity rise by 2.1X over ten years purely as a result of stated government policies being achieved.

If we put it in dollar terms, then the value of a $200,000 home would rise by $44,000 over ten years, solely from government policy. Because all of that would belong to the homeowner and none to the lender, that would be a 110% increase on the initial $40,000 in equity, which would more than double the portion of the homeowner's net worth that consists of equity in their home.

That isn't leverage in the ordinary sense. It is alignment with government policies and the multiplication of that alignment.

This is an amazing relationship, that has made a tremendous amount of money for many millions of homeowners over the decades, even if very few people think about it or are aware that it exists.

Aligning With The Government For A 10% Annual Gain

The government has an explicit goal of making everything (on average) cost around 2% more each year than it did the year before. The government has also been quite frequently forcing interest rates down to around 0%, particularly after the financial crisis of 2008, and then again with the pandemic of 2020.

If we earn nothing on our savings in the bank, but the prices of everything we buy is going up by about 2% per year - then as savers, we are losing about 2% of the value of our money in the bank every year. This annual loss for the savers of the nation is effectively a matter of national policy, simply as a result of the simultaneous goals for 2% inflation and 0% short term interest rates.

However, when we own a home with a mortgage, we can do something fascinating when it comes not to taking market risks

- but aligning ourselves with governmental policies, so that we profit from those policies.

The government intends for prices to rise by around 2% each year, as a matter of policy. This means that homes should go up by about 2% each year, all else being equal.

With an 80% LTV mortgage, the homeowner gets not only the 2% inflation gain for their own equity bucket - but the 2% gains for each of the four mortgage buckets as well. This means that every time the government succeeds in its annual objective of increasing price levels by 2% - *the homeowner sees their home equity increase by 10%.*

The very same policies that create a 2% annual loss in the value of what our savings in the bank will purchase, can also create a 10% annual gain in home equity as a matter of policy.

Now, that is not all of the Homeowner Wealth Formula - but it is a very powerful and stable base for the rest of the formula to build upon.

Just the government policy of attempting to make sure there is at least a 2% rate of inflation each year, by itself creates a 2.1X increase in home equity over 10 years.

When we take all inflation into account, including when inflation goes higher than what the government wants, then the historical record is an average 3X increase in home equity just from keeping with inflation alone.

When we also include mortgage amortization and changes in home prices that are not the result of inflation, then the historic national average for homeowners is to see their equity go up by 4.1X over ten years.

And the 2.1X wealth increase base for that remarkable history of homeowner wealth creation is not random, it is not gambling, and it is not speculation. Instead, it is alignment with a deliberate government policy of destroying the value of money and savings, reversing the usual negative outcome through the use of a home and mortgage, and turning that inflation into wealth in a way that multiplies the benefits for homeowners.

A History Of Halving & Doubling

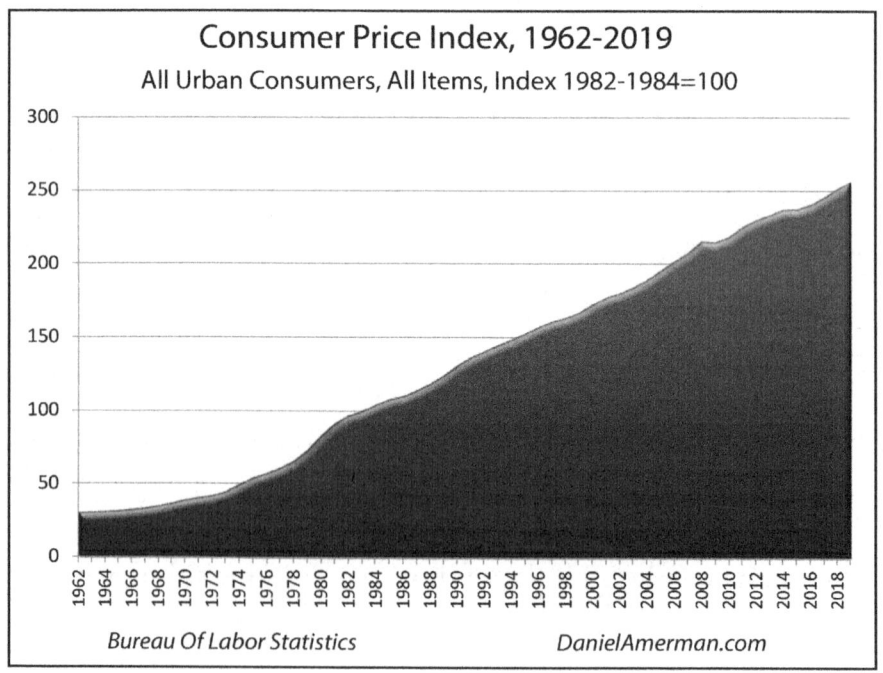

As reviewed in Chapter 2, when it comes to paying for the standard of living for the typical urban consumer, it took twice as many dollars in 1977 than it did in 1962, then twice again as many dollars by 1988, and then twice again as many dollars by 2016. In total, that is eight times the dollars, which means that for savers the value of their dollars would be only one eighth of what they started with.

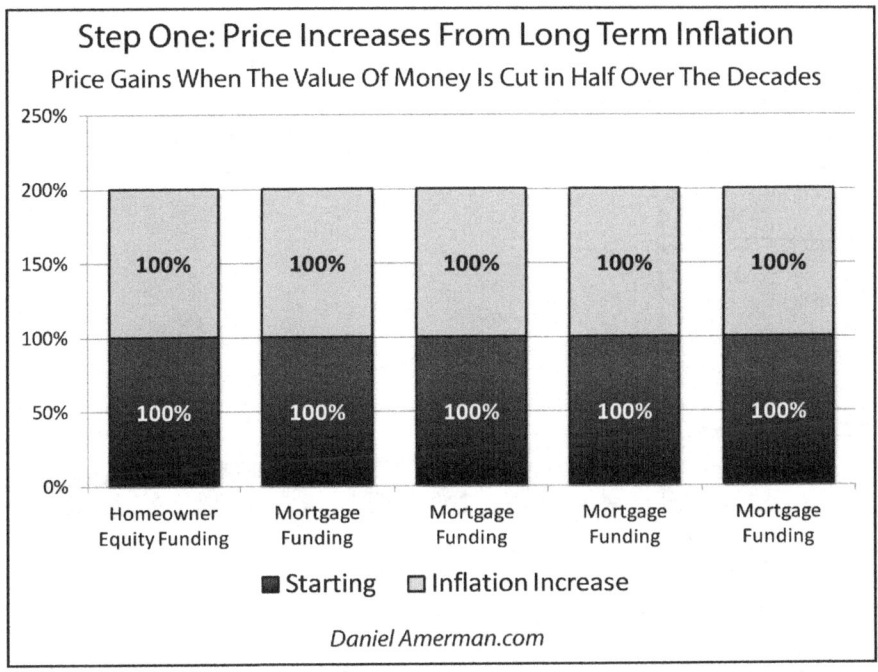

From a saver's perspective, or from the perspective of a retiree living on an annuity or pension that does not increase with inflation, that could be a quite depressing. However when we look at aligning ourselves with the destruction of the value of money, so that we can financially benefit from money losing half its value again and again over the years, then we can see a quite different flow of wealth over the years.

If we look at, say, 1962 to 1977, then on average it took twice as many dollars to pay for an average lifestyle in 1977 than it did in 1962. All it takes is homes merely keeping up with inflation, and that would mean that we would get a 100% gain on our equity investment.

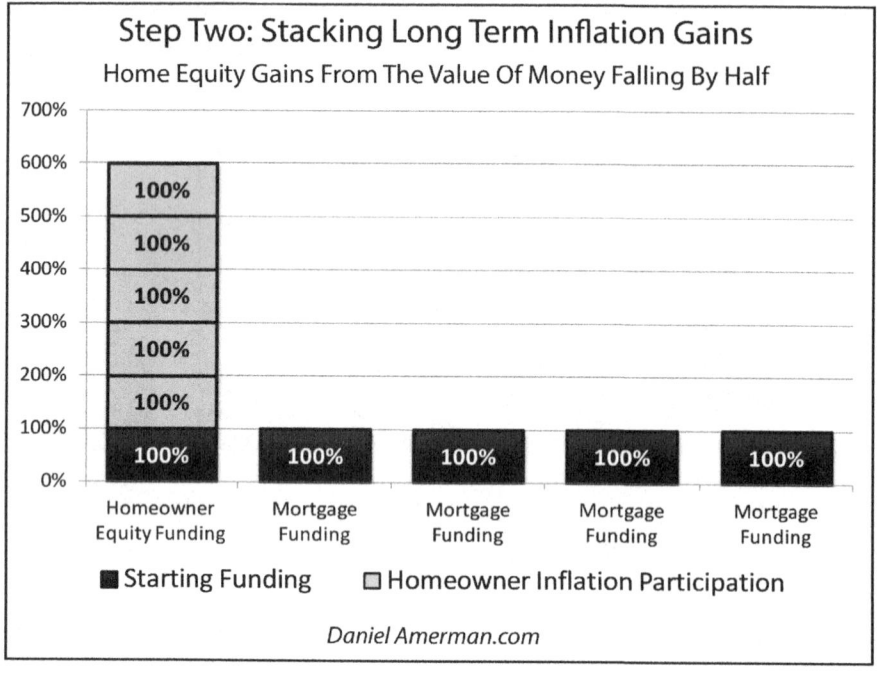

Thanks to our unequal partnership with the mortgage lender, we would also have had the rights to the entire 100% gain for each of the four buckets that represent the home purchase dollars put up by the lender. So we start with 100%, which is what we put up at closing, we double that for our equity share as the value of the dollar is cut in half and it takes twice as many dollars

The Homeowner Wealth Formula

to buy homes, and then we stack another four one hundred percents on top of that, which is the inflation based gains for all four of the mortgage lenders buckets, where they put the original money up but don't participate.

That stacking adds up to 600%, which can be phrased as our having 6 times the money we started with, or as a 500% gain on our original 100% in equity investment. And yes, the value of the dollar has been cut in half, but we have six times as many dollars. So, the natural flow of wealth over the decades is that as the overall population sees the value of their money cut in half again and again - each time that happens, homeowners with mortgages see their equity go up by six times, which leaves them with three times the purchasing power.

Now, there are other considerations over the course of many years, such as amortization, whether somebody moves or refinances, the details of the amount and LTV of the new mortgage, and so forth.

That said, the background force of $1 in equity becoming $6 in equity for homes purchased with 80% LTV mortgages each time the value of the dollar is cut in half is there in practice, and while the details may vary with each household, that wealth has been created again and again and again. This means that it can happen - and has happened - more than once over a lifetime, particularly if someone has several homes with several mortgages (or several investment properties).

Background: $1 → $6 while value of $1 to 50¢

As a simple illustration, someone (or everyone, on average) who bought a home in 1962 at age 25, would therefore have 6X their initial equity by age 40 in 1977, to the extent that their home just kept up with the rate of inflation.

If they had bought a new and larger home in that year, taking out a new 80% LTV mortgage, they would have had another 6X their initial equity by age 51 in 1988 - for a total of 36X their equity contribution at age 25.

That 36X increase in equity in 26 years is an astonishing number - but so is the historical fact of 75% of the purchasing power of the dollar being destroyed over 26 years.

Now, let's say the homeowner took just the compounded value of their initial equity, and bought a third home in 1988, at age 51. This would have to be a much nicer home, just because of the size of the equity, but to follow the numbers, let's say that they did, and they used another 80% LTV mortgage.

Between 1988 and 2016, the value of the dollar was cut in half again. It took twice as much to buy everything (on average) in 2016 than it did in 1988. And if we look at inflation only, that would twice as many dollars to buy (or sell) a comparable home in 2016.

Because of their buying a nicer home in 1988 with a new mortgage, they would have had another 6X their initial equity by age 79 in 2016 - for a total of 216X their equity contribution at age 25.

[handwritten: 30 yrs, 3 mort → 216X]

That 216 to 1 equity increase with three homes and three mortgages over the course of a lifetime is a fairly fantastic result - but it is history. And it is not just math, but repeated math - *keeping in mind that those increases in home prices are based on the compound interest formula, the increases in home equity are based on the five times multiplication of the power of compound interest, and the 216 to 1 equity increase is based on doing that five times multiplication, three times in a row.*

Steady annual rates of inflation are the first level of the multiplication of wealth. When fed into the compound interest formula, which is the second level of the multiplication of wealth, then inflation compounding inflation was sufficient to double the consumer price index between 1962 and 1977. For anyone who owned a home bought with an 80% mortgage in 1962, they would have been multiplying the power of compound interest with the third level of the multiplication of wealth, and they would have experienced a 6 to 1 increase. The same three levels of multiplication and the same 6 to 1 increase would also apply to homes bought in 1997, by the year 1988. The same three levels of multiplication and the same 6 to 1 increase would also apply to homes bought in 1988, by the year 2016.

Anyone who bought two homes with 80% LTV mortgages, in 1962 and 1977, would have had a 36X increase in initial equity

[handwritten: 1. Steady inflation 2. compound int & mort 3. repeat #2]

by 1988 (on average). Anyone who bought in 1977 and again in 1988 would have had the same 36X increase by 2016.

Those are the numbers, but getting too literal is not the idea here. There are many other factors to take into account, however the background force over the long term, is inflation creating wealth for homeowners in a major way and on a reliable basis. The specifics vary with the years, the mortgage LTVs and the locations, but there is no need to get all of the 36X or 216X increases in home equity - just getting a major piece of it is enough to be life changing, and indeed, has been life changing for millions of people over the decades.

The Longer Term National History Of A Wealth Creation Engine

What set the stage for the reliability of inflation creating wealth for homeowners was when the U.S. dollar went off the gold standard for domestic purposes in 1933, after the inauguration of President Franklin Roosevelt and in the depths of the Great Depression. The reason was to be able to induce inflation, as the gold-backed dollar was then stuck in a round of deflation, growing more valuable each year, and this was believed to be contributing to the economic depression. So the U.S. and most other developed nations all went off the gold standard for domestic purposes in the early 1930s.

The Homeowner Wealth Formula

The United States was indeed able to almost immediately break the back of deflation - where it took ever fewer gold backed dollars each year to buy things. Even in the depths of a depression the government (through the Federal Reserve) was able to promptly create a round of inflation with the new purely paper dollars, where it took ever more dollars to buy everything.

As history has shown since 1933, if a nation has a purely paper (or electronic) currency that isn't tied to anything tangible in value, and it has a stated policy of at least slightly reducing the value of its own currency every year - then they can be highly effective at this, creating a long, one way street of the destruction the currency, halving the purchasing power again and again over the decades, as the number of dollars needed to buy everything doubles and doubles again.

Since 1933, the purchasing power of the U.S. dollar has fallen by about 95%, partially by accident, but much of it was through an entirely deliberate government policy of trying to ensure there are at least low to moderate rates of inflation in each year. This process has been terrible for the value of savings or for pensions or salaries that don't keep up with inflation, but it has had a quite different impact on homeowners, particularly for those with mortgages. Through a long, relentless, and quite reliable process over the many decades, it now takes about 20 times as many dollars to pay for everything (on average) compared to what it did in 1933.

For homes over the longer term, we can see a good example of how this process has worked if we look at what the Census Bureau can tell us about home prices. According to the U.S. Census Bureau, with the data collected from their ten year censuses, the median value of a single family home in the United States was:

$2,938 in 1940;

$7,354 in 1950;

$11,900 in 1960;

$17,000 in 1970;

$47,200 in 1980;

$79,100 in 1990; and

$119,600 in 2000.

The Census Bureau has changed what and how it reports since the 2000 census, however, results from the Federal Reserve's 2010 and 2019 *Survey of Consumer Finances* can be used as (approximate) substitutes. According to the Federal Reserve, the median value of a single family home in the United States was:

$170,600 in 2010; and

$225,000 in 2019.

The Homeowner Wealth Formula

The Census Bureau and Federal Reserve numbers are not quite as good as the Freddie Mac Home Price Index numbers used in the rest of this book, because they don't take into consideration changing home sizes and amenities, or population shifts to more expensive urban areas. However, those are just adjustments, the broad strokes of our shared story are still valid and they are overwhelming.

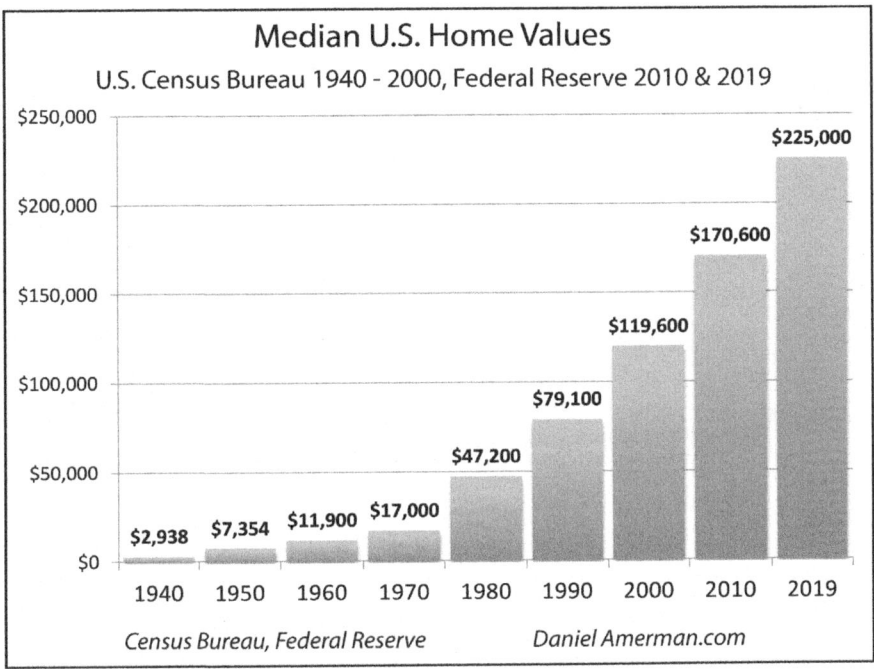

For a reader today, those numbers may seem surreal and almost too small to be believed - particularly the $2,938 in 1940 or the $17,000 even as recently as 1970 - but that is the point. The multiplication in home values that occurs over the decades is entirely real and it is consistent - even if the speed may vary with the particular decade.

7% doubles every 10 years

Going back to 1940 (and before):

1) History shows us many decades of inflation multiplying the number of paper dollars it takes to buy almost all things - including hard assets such as homes - using the full power of the compound interest formula;

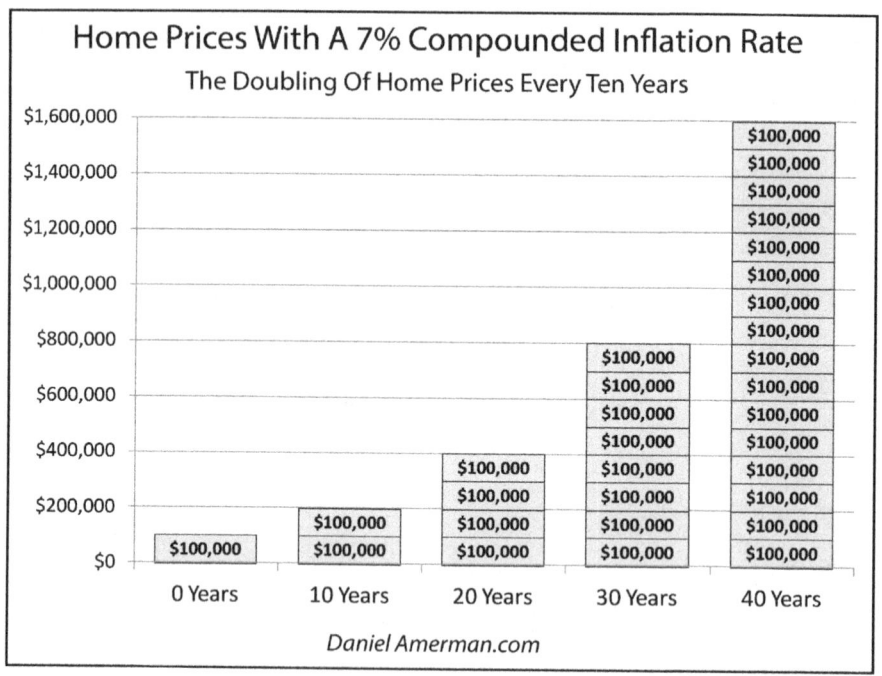

Indeed, if our historical home price graph looked familiar, it should, because it's just the real world results of the application of the compound interest formula for home prices we developed in Chapter 3. The rates of inflation were variable in practice and quite a bit lower than 7% on average, so there were more decades involved than with our round number example, but the actual shape of the graph of housing prices over the decades is very similar to a simple compound interest example.

The Homeowner Wealth Formula

With the 7% compound interest example, the price of a home rose by 16X over 40 years. The actual history of median home values in the U.S. was a 77X increase over about 80 years. The predominant and overwhelming driver of home prices in the United States over the decades has been a process of steady and relentless inflation compounding upon itself over the years, with the result of home prices doubling again and again and again over the decades.

2) When we buy a home that is mostly initially paid for with someone else's money (the mortgage lender), and then multiply the benefits from keeping all of inflation based price gains for ourselves, we have a multiplication of what is primarily compound interest. What long term homeownership comes down to then is starting with the most powerful and reliable source of wealth creation in history, that of compound interest, and then multiplying the power of compound interest because of the unequal partnership between the homeowner and the mortgage lender.

3) The historically average result of this remarkable multiplication of the power of compound interest is an astonishing increase in the amount of the original equity contribution.

4) Going back 80 years, as far back as we can go with ten year census results and a dollar that is not directly backed by gold, this multiplication of compound interest has produced

major increases in home prices, and then much greater increases in home equity - every decade and without exception. It is an even more powerful source of wealth creation every two decades, meaning it is likely to happen multiple times for a single individual over the course of their lifetimes.

Those four steps are not all of the Homeowner Wealth Formula, but they do form the core of the wealth creation, and the historically proven core of the reliability of the wealth creation over the long term.

As a simple example, when we look at just the census bureau numbers, the key then is not just the move from an average home price of $2,938 in 1940 to $7,354 in 1950 - attractive though that was. Instead it was putting 20% down, or $588, to own all of the rights to the $4,416 increase in home prices that would occur over the next 10 years.

Not including mortgage amortization, the homeowners of the nation would have gone from owning a $2,938 home with a $2,350 mortgage, to owning a $7,354 home with a $2,350 mortgage. Their equity would increase from $588 in 1940 to $5,004 in 1950. That means they would have 852% of the home equity in 1950, or 8.5X the home equity that they did in 1940.

The Homeowner Wealth Formula

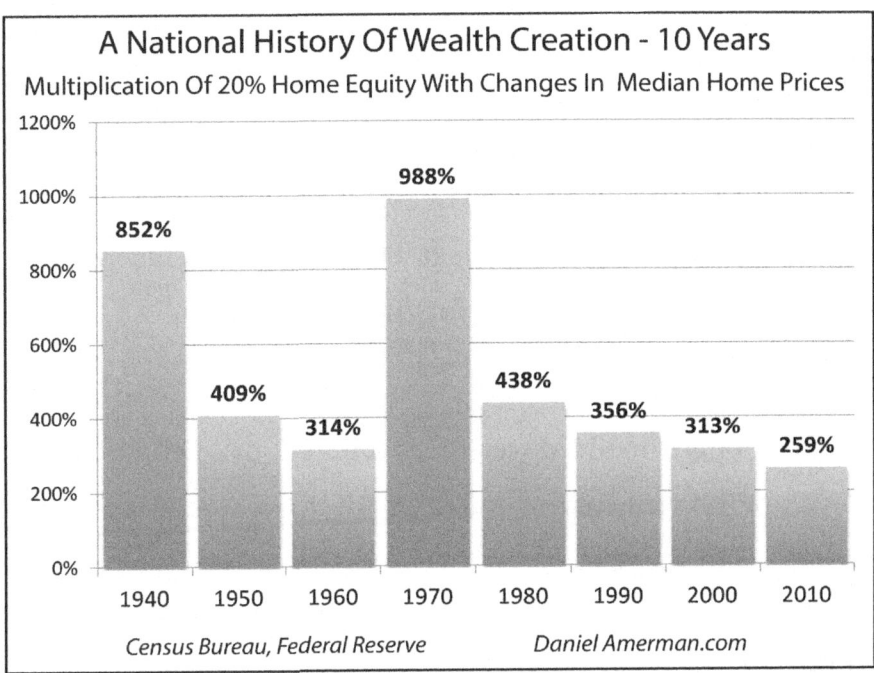

What the graph of the national history of wealth creation shows is a series of astonishing increases in home equity. Now, to be clear - these are broad strokes, because we don't have the same quality of data going back to 1940 like we do going back to 1975, so we don't have the exactly comparable homes, or the mortgage rates, or the split between inflation and market value changes for comparable homes. Those are adjustments, but that is all they are, modifications for an enormously powerful flow of wealth.

With that understood - this is in broad strokes the history of homeownership for the entire nation, for almost the entire period that the federal government has been dedicated to destroying at least a bit of the value of a paper dollar year. Over the years, this has created a potent form of compound interest, which the homeowners who bought homes with mortgages have been able to consistently multiply when it comes to their home equity.

When median home prices for the entire nation increased from $7,354 in 1950 to $11,900 in 1960 - for someone who had bought their home in 1950 with an 80% LTV mortgage, they would have seen their home equity increase by about 4.1X over just ten years.

The dollars involved were very different by 1980 - because so much of the value of the dollar was destroyed between 1950 and 1980 - but the relationships were the same. The median home value went from $47,200 in 1980 to $79,100 in 1990. This meant that the natural and expected outcome for buying a home with a mortgage anywhere in the nation in the year 1980, was to see their home equity increase by about 4.4X in just those ten years.

Sometimes the increases were greater, as in the remarkable almost 10X increase over the 1970s, for those who were able to flip that decade's destructively high rates of inflation into multiplied wealth. Sometimes the increases were less, as in the 3.1X home equity increase for those who bought in 2000, or the 2.6X nine year increase for those buying in 2010. However, all were not just positive, but were remarkably positive.

The Homeowner Wealth Formula

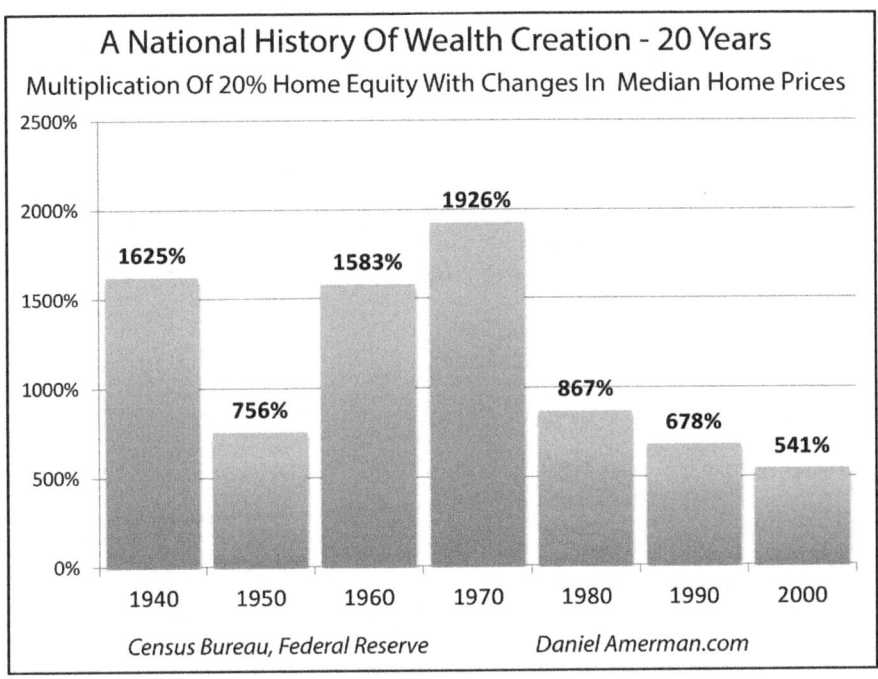

The strength and consistency of the wealth creation becomes even stronger still when we move out to the national average experience for owning a home for 20 years. The peak is now an almost 20X increase in home equity, for those who bought homes with mortgages at the median value of $17,000 in 1970, with $3,400 down, and still owned them at the $79,100 median home value in 1990. Indeed, the increase would be larger still if we were including 20 years of mortgage amortization, which we are not (at this point in the book).

The increases are not quite of that magnitude in other years, but nonetheless, when inflation is given twenty years to run and compound, and that result is then multiplied because of unequal partnership - the national history of home equity increases is still stunning. This is true whether we are looking at the near 16X increases in the twenty years after 1940 and 1960, or the near 8X increases after 1950 or 1980.

Quaint Home Prices & Future Home Prices

For many of the decades shown, the home prices are so low as to seem quaint, but that is some ways the most important part of all. What history shows us is that just from inflation alone, at some time in the future today's home prices are going to look astonishing cheap, to the point they are difficult to relate to. Just as we might look back now and say "Buy a home for just $12,000? That's nuts!", at some point in the future, people are likely to say "Buy a home for just $225,000? That's nuts!".

Over the course of a lifetime, with only the speed varying, what a dollar will buy repeatedly halves from $1, to fifty cents to 25 cents, to 12 1/2 cents.

Over the course of a lifetime, with only the speed varying, the number of dollars it takes to buy things (including homes) multiplies from $1, to $2, to $4, to $8.

Over the course of a lifetime, for someone who buys three homes over time with 80% LTV mortgages (all else being equal), then with the multiplication of the multiplication, $1 becomes $6, which becomes $36, which then becomes $216.

The Homeowner Wealth Formula

The specifics are not likely to work out in exactly that way, and there are many other considerations. There is no need to go multiple rounds, the LTVs can change, and the mortgage can be paid off. Those can each still lead to highly positive outcomes, regardless, although not the 36 to 1 or 216 to 1 shown. Because the numbers are so great, there is no need to capture all of it - or even most of it - in order to still have potentially life changing results when it comes to net worth and financial security.

What matters is that behind everything else is the background force, the natural flow of wealth that is at work.

That isn't gambling. That isn't playing the market. That isn't risky leveraged investing in the way that most people use the term. Over a sufficiently long term, with national averages, this is more a matter of alignment with a fundamental, foundational force.

What has been reviewed in this chapter is not theory and it isn't speculation. It is the story of a nation.

The steady multiplication of home prices using the compound interest formula is what we, our parents and our grandparents all lived, or at least for those whose parents and grandparents were homeowners and who lived in the United States. And the multiplication of the compound interest formula results for those who bought homes with mortgages was the completely natural result, potentially happening repeatedly over the decades, with several homes or refinancings. This was true even if the homeowners involved had no idea of the fundamental financial and economic forces that were making them "house rich", with soaring home equities - because this powerful engine of steadily turning inflation into wealth was the natural outcome, they didn't need to know.

Now, national averages are not necessarily individual experiences, particularly over shorter time periods and in particular locations. There are certainly ways of losing money, and many individuals have most certainly done so with shorter time frames or in specific distressed locations. However, the overwhelming majority of the homeownership experience in the United States has been substantially positive, and these very positive results have historically usually happened fairly quickly.

Chapter 6

A 99.7% Chance Of Earning 5X The Money

In the previous two chapters we explored the history of inflation and housing prices, and developed the underlying heart of the Homeowner Wealth Formula, which is the *multiplication* of the *multiplication*, the multiplication of the power of compound interest.

The government, in the form of the Federal Reserve, has a policy of multiplying the number of dollars that it takes to buy, well - almost anything - over time. If the Fed meets its approximate target, then the prices of everything are multiplied times 1.02 each year, so that what cost $100 one year costs $102 the next year, and $122 in ten years.

Inflation meant that between 1962 and 2016, what originally cost $1 later cost $2, and then $4, and then $8. As the cost of homes has historically been closely tied to inflation, this progression applied to homes as well.

This then raises the question - just how reliable is that process?

Is this just leverage, and rolling the dice? If the odds are in our favor - then how strongly are they in our favor?

If this is to be a natural flow of wealth, one of the requirements is that just being there in a particular position, with no particular skills or luck, should be enough on average to bring in a substantially positive result. When we look at the historical averages for how a home with a mortgage turns inflation into wealth - simply being in the position of being a homeowner certainly meets that test, no special skill or luck needed.

Another desirable attribute of a natural flow of wealth is that it should be forgiving. Negative outcomes can be possible, but there should be a wide range of results that are below average, perhaps as the result of bad luck or poor execution - but that are still pretty good, or at least OK.

Ordinarily - this should keep what are usually called leveraged strategies from being a natural flow of wealth. Because all else being equal, leveraged strategies involve a significant risk of a catastrophic outcome - and that degree of risk exposure would keep them from being a natural flow of wealth.

The Homeowner Wealth Formula

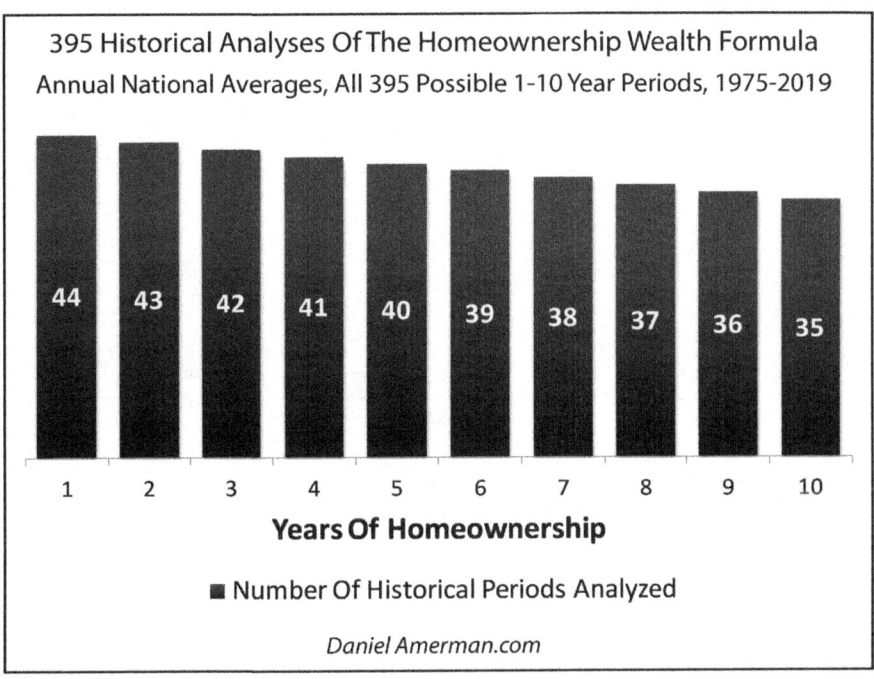

To see the risk when it comes to multiplying the multiplication - keeping it to inflation only in this section - then we have 395 possible 1-10 year homeownership periods between 1975 and 2019.

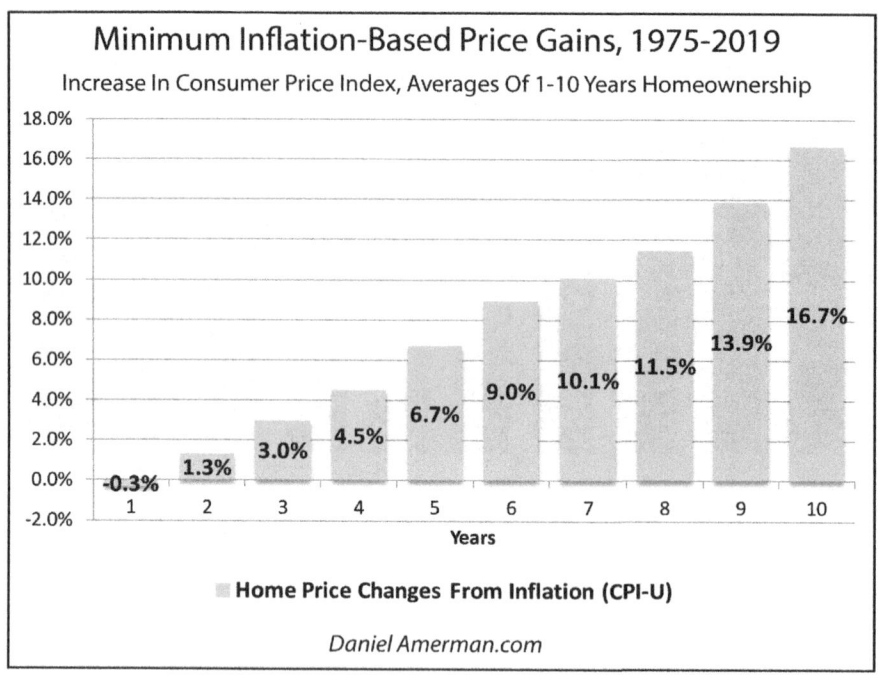

When we look at the number of times that inflation failed to deliver, and prices got cheaper instead of higher - then according to U.S. government statistics, there was only one year that happened. This was between 2008 and 2009, when the rate of inflation was -0.3%, which meant that it only took 99.7 cents to buy in 2009 what had taken $1 to buy in 2008. (And yes, home prices dropped by much more than 0.3% in 2009, which will be covered in detail in Book #2, but in this first book we are still isolating the magnitude and reliability of the primary underlying wealth drivers of inflation and mortgages.)

Except for that one very small exception, the other 394 possible 1-10 year homeownership periods all experienced positive rates of inflation. When we look at the historical odds that a homeowner would experience positive inflation then, with more dollars being required to buy everything on average (including houses), the odds are 394/395, which equals 99.7%.

To have the odds be 99.7% in our favor is fairly amazing - and it goes back to the difference between aligning ourselves with government policies, versus rolling the dice in a casino or speculating in the markets.

United States dollars have no inherent value, they are not worth anything by themselves, unlike say, gold, silver, gemstones, food or land. All that gives value to the dollar is the backing by the United States government. And when the only underlying source of value for the dollar is a government that as an open matter of policy is dedicated to slowly destroying the value of the dollar each year - history shows that it is highly, highly reliable at accomplishing this, with a 99.7% success rate.

Multiplying Very Low Rates Of Inflation

With an 80% LTV mortgage, what happens with very low rates of inflation? How badly are homeowners hurt if they are so unfortunate as to own homes during a time when money is doing a particularly poor job of losing value?

To answer, let's take a look at the lowest rate of inflation experienced out of all 43 possible two year homeownership periods, which was 2008 to 2010. Prices rose by 1.3%, meaning it (on average) took $101.30 in 2010 to buy what would have cost $100.00 in 2008.

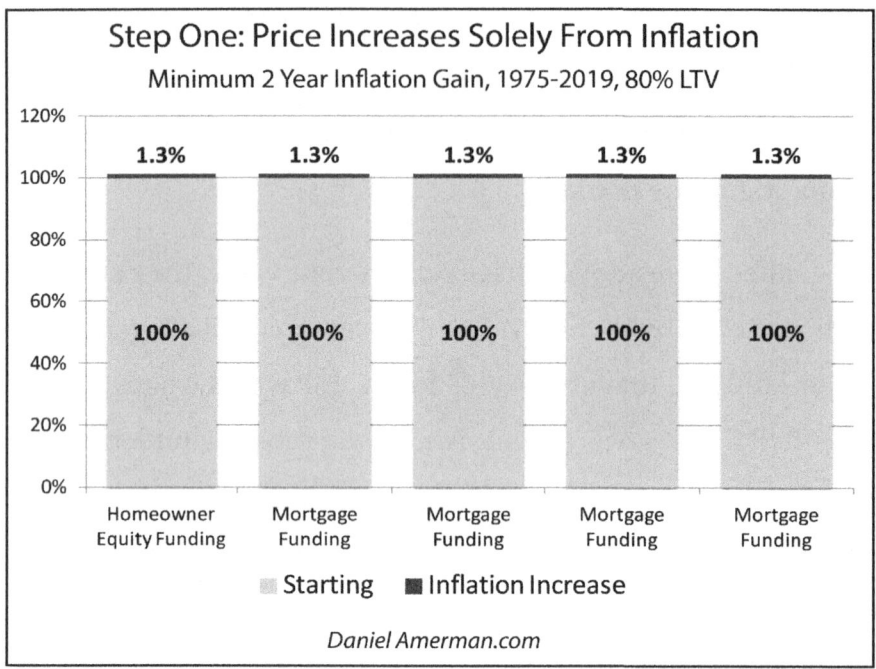

The homeowner would have been entitled to their 1.3% inflation price gain. Because of the unequal partnership, the homeowner would also be entitled to the other four 1.3% inflation based gains as well.

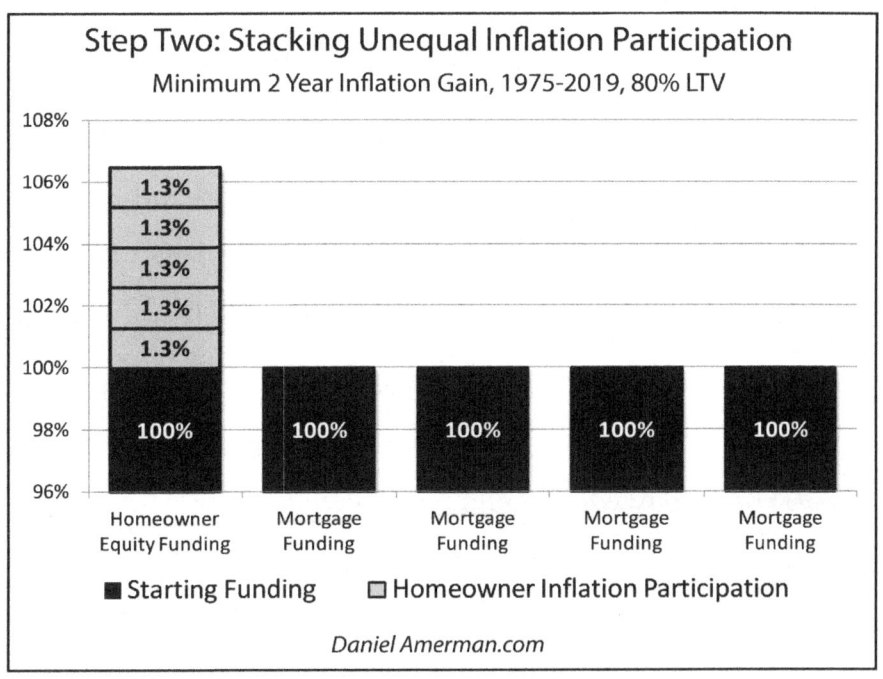

All five of the 1.3% inflation gains stack on top of each other, and the homeowner gains 6.5% on their $40,000 home equity contribution over the two years.

With an example $200,000 home, the 1.3% gain on $40,000 in equity is equal to $520. Stack the other four $520 gains on top, and the total 6.5% gain on equity is worth $2,600.

Now, a $2,600 inflation gain on $40,000 in equity over two years is not as exciting as some of the numbers we previously reviewed. This small but nice gain does however needs to be put in perspective - it is the minimum out of all 43 historical two year periods, it is the *worst case* when we look at the primary underlying wealth drivers of inflation requiring more dollars to buy homes, a non-amortizing debt, and the unequal partnership.

The worst case with just those factors is five times the money. And all 42 other possibilities between 1975 and 2019 also worked to be five times the money, it was just five times more money every other time.

Another way of looking at this is that using an average 2% inflation target, the government would have intended for it to take $104.04 to buy what would have taken $100 two years earlier. The government failed, and in this case it was the worst two year failure over all those decades, with the actual price increase being only $101.30. But nonetheless, the result for an exceptionally unlucky homeowner aligning their financial interests with the government during the two worst available years - was to still see a multiplication of the dollars needed to buy a home, and to still experience a multiplication of a multiplication that went to their benefit in the form of increased home equity.

Five Times The Gain, 99.7% Of The Time

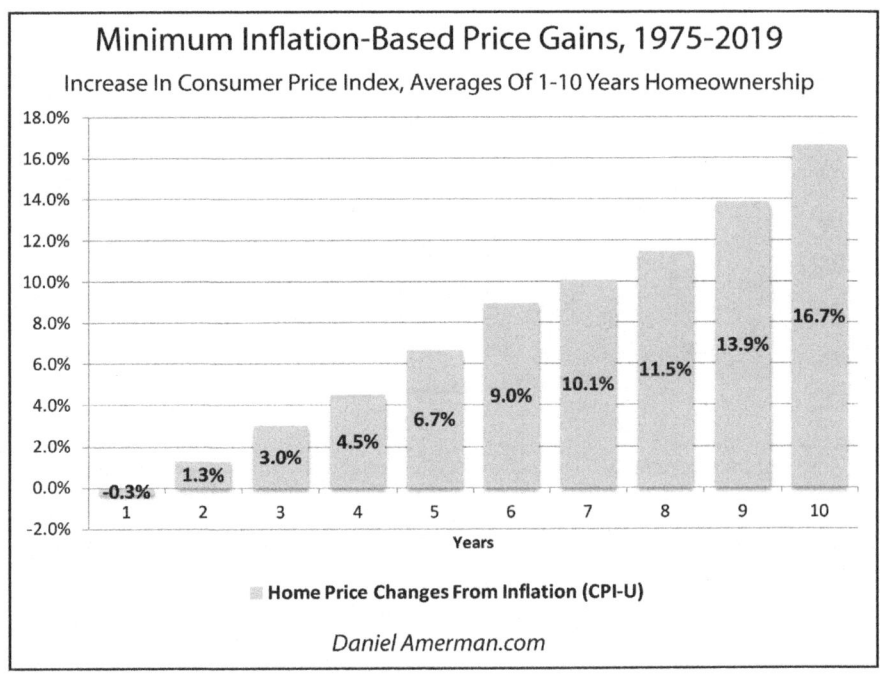

This ability to multiply times five applies up and down the scale, for all 395 possible 1-10 year holding periods.

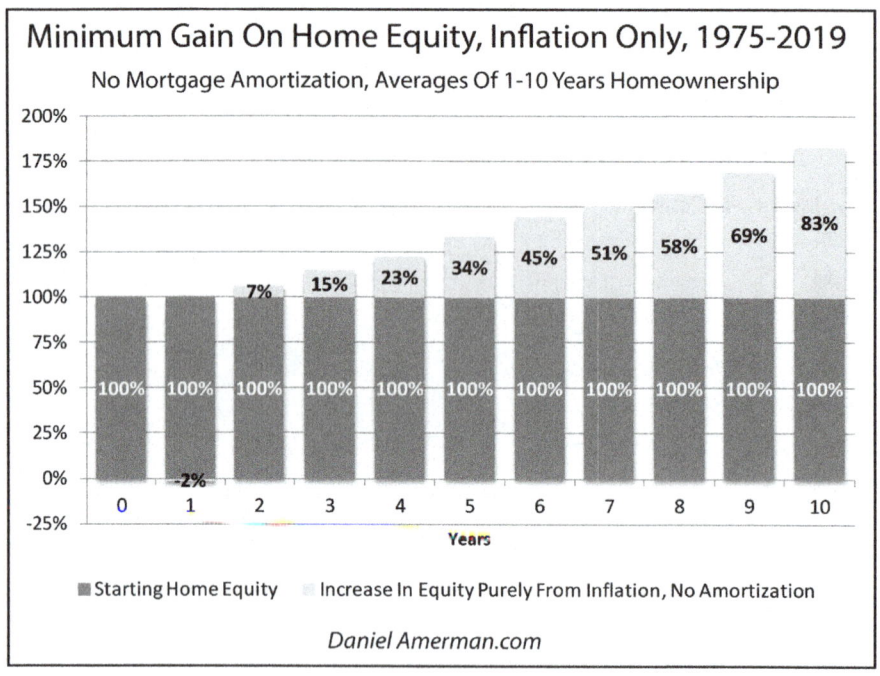

There is only one negative number for inflation (one year of deflation), and as with the gains, we multiply the loss times five. So -0.3% times five is a 1.5% loss over the course of one year (rounded to -2% in the graph above), which would be a dollar loss of $600 on $40,000 in equity.

Everywhere else is a positive multiplied times a positive. The minimum out of all 42 of the 3 year periods was to see prices rise by only 3%, as can be seen in the upper graph. This means the minimum inflation-based gain on home equity with a non-amortizing mortgage was five times that, or 15% over 3 years, as can be seen in the lower graph.

When we go to five years, the minimum inflation-based increase in price levels out of the 40 possibilities is 6.7%. Multiply times five, and the worst case (from these underlying factors alone) is a 34% gain on home equity over five years.

Increasing Reliability Over Time

As developed in Chapter 3, what is also crucial is to note how much more reliable inflation becomes over time - which then increases the reliability of a significant gain from the multiplication of that inflation.

Very low rates of inflation are a failure by the government from a policy perspective. The government is very, very good at making the value of money go down each year, and the number of dollars needed to buy things - including homes - go up each year. The more time the government has to work, the more reliable the cumulative destruction of the purchasing power of the dollar, and the less the power of a single year of low inflation to pull things down.

The other process is that the more time that passes, the greater the value of the multiplication of the multiplication. So when we go out ten years, the single "worst" result from inflation, and ten successive years of needing more money to buy things, is a 16.7% price increase. Take that, multiply times five (for an 80%

LTV mortgage), and the result is a quite respectable 83% increase in equity over ten years - as the worst result. With the other 34 ten year outcomes from these underlying wealth drivers all being better, and most of them being much better.

A 100% Success Rate, With 5X The Wealth - But No Guarantees

It is entirely accurate to say that when we look at the wealth drivers explored in this chapter, that 394 out of 395 of the 1-10 year historical periods led to positive outcomes, which is a 99.7% success rate. It is also accurate to say that with an 80% LTV mortgage (as an example), that the positive outcome would have been multiplied by five, every one of those 394 times.

More impressively, if we go out another year and look at all 351 of the 2-10 year homeownership periods between 1975 and 2019 - every one of them was positive. That is a 100% success rate, with two or more years of inflation. Each of those 351 successes would be multiplied times five, in the multiplication of the multiplication.

Now, that is in no way a guarantee for any one homeowner or real estate investor.

The Homeowner Wealth Formula

These are not yet all the factors. Inflation, a non-amortizing mortgage, and the unequal partnership are the primary underlying wealth drivers, that combination has been 100% positive over all 2+ year periods, and they do explain an average 3 to 1 increase in equity over ten years of home ownership, which is the majority of the 4.1 to 1 increase that is the national average outcome for all the tens of millions of homeowners over the decades.

But that said, when we add in all the rest of factors that increase the gains to that 4.1 to 1 - a lot more variability is brought into play. Not all years are positive. There is also the issue with national averages. This is indeed the average experience - it is the best information we have for the nation as a whole - but there is a tremendous amount of variability when it comes to specific metro areas, specific neighborhoods and specific homes, which can create widely varying individual outcomes.

What we explored here was the shifting of the odds that can occur when we make life choices that align ourselves with what most people would view as a destructive government policy, turn that policy to our personal financial advantage, and then multiply the results.

The outcomes are not random - but are highly, highly reliable and consistent. They aren't everything - but there are very few ways to get a even a somewhat reliable five to one increase, and there are even fewer ways to get it 100% of the time. To have this critical and extraordinary historical record not as the whole formula, but as the base to work from, is an entirely different way of thinking for most people. Hopefully this chapter has been helpful to the reader in seeing inflation and opportunities in a quite different light.

Chapter 7

Turning High Inflation Into Rapid Wealth Creation

There is more to inflation than just alignment with government policies. Sometimes inflation will go out of control, climbing far above where the government wants it to go, often for many years. This rapid and sustained destruction of the value of money can be devastating for the economy and financial markets.

On a personal level, it can be very difficult for savers to keep up with inflation, and much or most of the value of their savings can be wiped out for millions of people. High rates of inflation can be particularly cruel for older workers and for those who have already retired. Their savings get destroyed and the remaining working years (if any) simply aren't there for many older people to rebuild what they lost, leaving them with far less financial security than what they thought they had achieved over a lifetime of working.

As we will explore in this chapter, for many people the single best feature of the Homeowner Wealth Formula is its relationship with high rates of inflation, when the value of money is being rapidly destroyed for a nation.

One aspect of this is simply the creation of wealth - the higher the rate of inflation, then the faster that real wealth is created for homeowners. Indeed, if someone owns a home with a mortgage in their younger years, and a round of high inflation hits, then the degree of profits is so great that it can give them financial security for decades thereafter. This isn't just theory, but something that has worked for tens of millions of households in the past, even if few were fully aware of the particulars of the source of their new but accidental prosperity.

Rapidly creating wealth is always good, but for many people - particularly for those who are a bit older - it is the source of the creation of wealth that is even more important. High rates of inflation are enormously destructive, for both the nation and personal financial security. The nature of the Homeowner Wealth Formula is to reverse the negative effects of inflation and turn inflation into wealth instead.

For many households - the higher the rate of inflation, the more the damage that is done to their savings, and the greater the hit to their financial security. For a homeowner with a mortgage, however - the higher the rate of inflation, the more wealth that is created. This creates a natural but enormously powerful offset - a hedge - that can otherwise be almost impossible for an ordinary person to obtain.

Crucially, for a home with a mortgage, it isn't just that the value of the home is protected from inflation. Instead, as we have been reviewing, we have something much better which is a multiplication of the multiplication, and this multiplied wealth in the form of radically increased home equity can then offset - or more than offset - inflation damage elsewhere when it comes to savings or other financial assets.

This natural flow of wealth can then protect the net worth of the homeowner on an inflation-adjusted basis. It is also simply unavailable to renters, who do not gain from inflation, but are fully exposed to fast rising rental payments.

Three Times The Money In Three Years

To see an example of how this can work, and just how swift and powerful the Homeowner Wealth Formula can be in turning inflation into wealth, let's look at the three years from 1978 to 1981.

We're still keeping this very simple, so we are just looking at the underlying wealth drivers of inflation, a non-amortizing mortgage, and an unequal partnership. Our first multiplication is the rate of inflation increasing the number of dollars needed to buy almost everything - including homes. Comparing average prices as measured by the Consumer Price Index, it took about 40% more dollars to buy things in 1981 than in 1978, which inflicted enormous damage on savers and the nation.

All five of the buckets go up, with a 40% gain on the 20% of the home purchase we funded with our own money, and 40% on each of the 20% buckets funded by the mortgage lender.

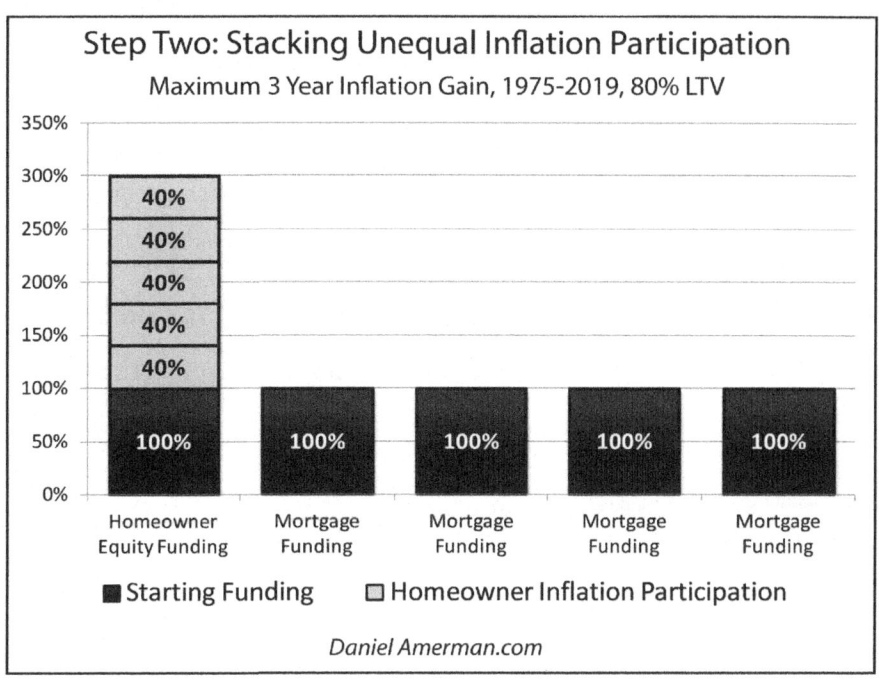

Because of the unequal partnership, we keep all the gains, and the bank gets none. We stack the five 40% gains on top of each other, and we get the entire 200% gain relative our starting home equity investment. In other words, after three years - we would have 3 times the money.

For a $200,000 home, our 20% starting equity would have been $40,000. The 40% gain on our bucket would be worth $16,000 - with the same $16,000 gains on the other four buckets. Stacking them up, that is $80,000 in gains, which brings the home equity total up to $120,000. That is indeed three times the money, in just three years.

The way that most people look at the world, and comparing this to investments, savings or the price of almost anything as reported in the media - three times the money is entirely accurate, and there is no need to go beyond that.

That said, because the value of money is falling fast, it could be argued that the most important number is not the dollars, but the purchasing power of the new dollars in equity. From a professional perspective, in my opinion this type of analysis needs to always be run simultaneously in nominal and inflation-adjusted dollars when it comes to real estate (or just about any other kind of long term investment). For a serious investor or someone who is trying to shield significant savings from inflation, there is no substitute for rolling up one's sleeves and getting into a more complete understanding of the critical factors that are in play.

However, that sets up unnecessary screens for an average person who is just thinking of buying or refinancing a home, and we can take a much simpler shortcut instead.

We end up with 3 times the starting dollars, or 300%. By that time it costs 40% more to buy things, which is 140% of where we started. Simply divide the 300% by the 140%, and that is 214%, i.e. 2.14 times our starting money. When we look at what happened in purchasing power terms, and adjust for inflation, we have still more than doubled the real value of our money in just three short years, by flipping to our advantage the same force that was wreaking havoc on savings, bonds, pensions and annuities.

(Another way of doing this is to say that the purchasing power of $1.00 fell to 71 cents because of the high rate of inflation, and if we take the 300% and multiply it by 71%, we get an inflation-adjusted result of 214% of starting equity. Two conceptual paths to the same number, they both work.)

Crucially, if there was no mortgage, then the value of the home goes up by 40% to 140%, the price to purchase everything goes up by 40% to 140%, we divide 140% by 140%, and we get one. The house keeps up with inflation - which is much better than not keeping up with inflation - but there is no real gain. To turn inflation into wealth we do need all the components of inflation, a home, and the mortgage that provides both much of the funding for the home purchase, as well as the unequal partnership for the gains resulting from inflation.

Maximum Wealth Creation

The three year historical example shown consisted of the three years with the highest rate of inflation experienced, out of the 42 three year periods between 1975 and 2019.

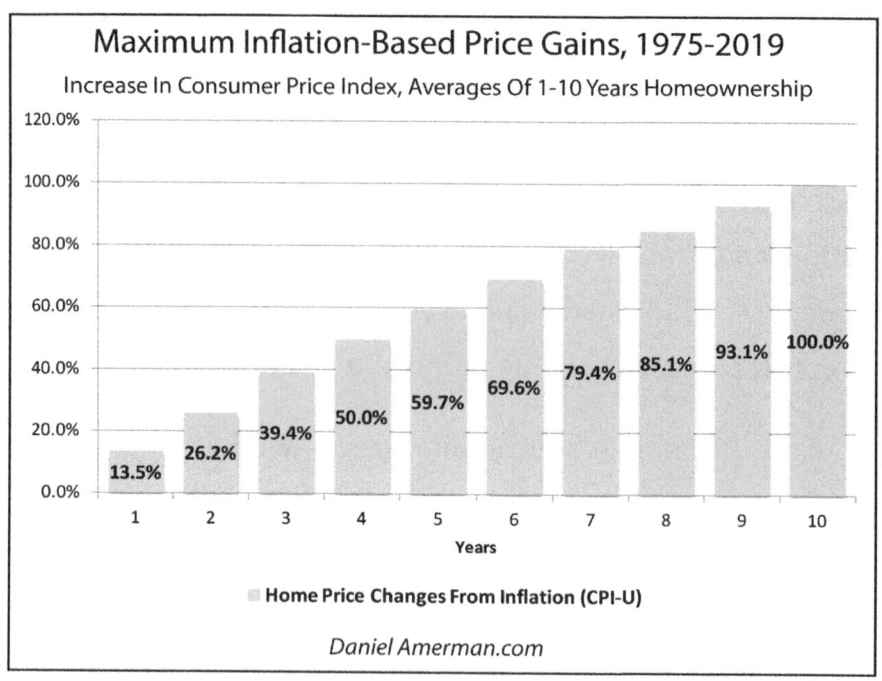

When we look at the highest rates of inflation for each of the 1-10 year homeownership periods, then we get the graph above. The biggest rates of inflation - and the maximum historical destruction of the value of the dollar - were a 50% increase in the number of dollars needed to purchase things in four years, about an 80% increase in 7 years, and a 100% increase in ten years.

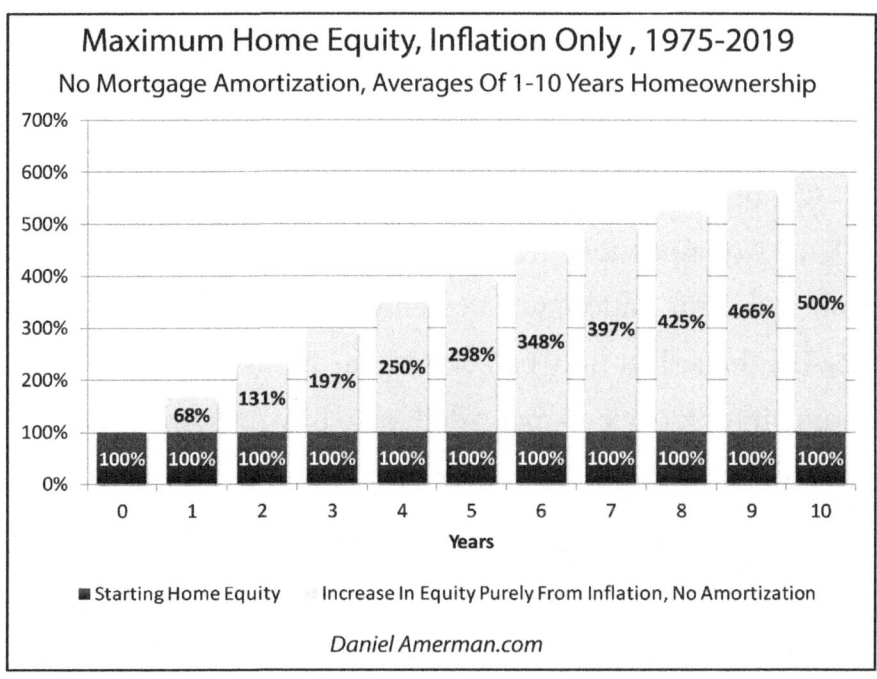

When we stack the gains up from the unequal partnership, and do our second multiplication times five (assuming an 80% non-amortizing mortgage), we get the graph above of maximum gains on home equity from inflation only.

Take the maximum 60% gain over five years (rounded) that occurred between 1986 and 1981, multiply times five, and that is about a 300% gain. Stack the 300% gain on top of the 100% starting equity, and that is four times the money - in a mere five years.

There was an approximate 80% gain in the Consumer Price Index between 1975 and 1982. That worst possible time period for savers - provided homeowners with 5 times the money, in just seven years. The worse it gets with inflation destroying the value of money - the better the job the Homeowner Wealth Formula does of turning inflation into wealth.

Out of all 395 of the 1-10 year periods between 1975 and 2019, the worst possible period for savers, retirees on fixed incomes, and the nation, was the ten years between 1975 and 1985. The dollar lost fully half of its value in just ten years, meaning it took twice as many dollars to buy most things in 1985 than it did in 1975.

This same dreadful decade for savers, when fed into the three underlying wealth drivers of inflation, a home with a non-amortizing mortgage, and the unequal partnership - produced the best results of any one of the 395 possible 1-10 periods.

The Homeowner Wealth Formula

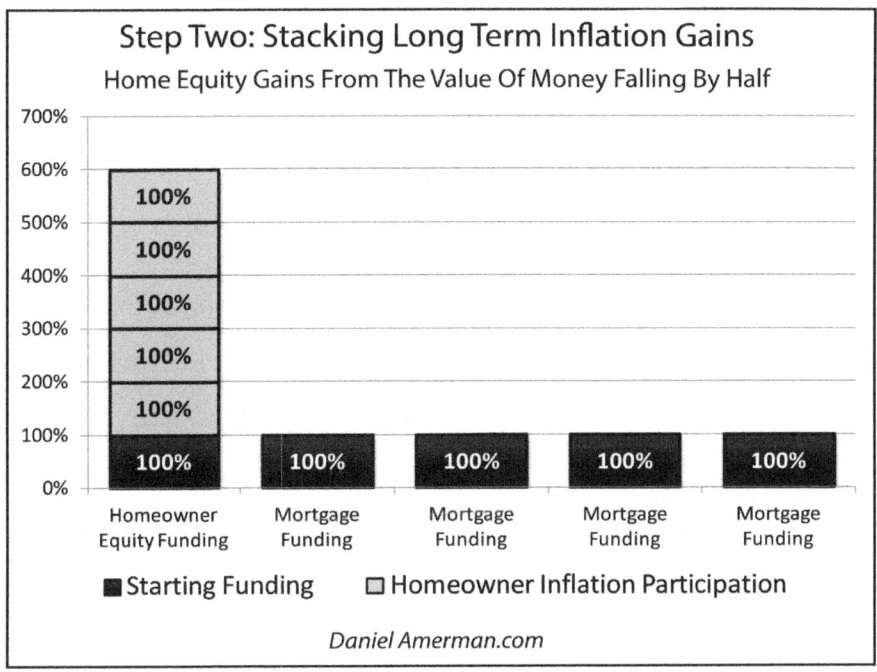

The worse everything else gets - the better the results that the Homeowner Wealth Formula delivers. In this case a 50% decline in the value of dollar, when we go through both multiplications, becomes a six times increase in the amount of home equity, in just ten years.

Crucially, the best possible 6 to 1 growth in home equity was also the best possible increase in inflation-adjusted net worth, out of all 395 possibilities. The numbers are fairly simple. There were six times the dollars of home equity after ten years, with each dollar being worth half as much, so the homeowner had 3 times the purchasing power, even after discounting for a very destructive high rate of inflation.

This is very rare and very crucial. The worse that the destruction of the value of the dollar becomes, the greater the amount of after-inflation wealth that is created. For someone who is relatively young, this rapid compounding of net worth can set the base for a lifetime of substantially enhanced financial security.

For someone a bit older who is concerned about protecting what they have, the Homeowner Wealth Formula doesn't just keep up with inflation, as do most inflation hedges. Instead it generates so much money, that it can effectively reach out and protect the value of other savings or investments, potentially protecting much of the entire net worth of the saver from inflation, and not just the amount invested in home equity.

Accidental Prosperity & Toy Mortgages

The ability to turn high rates of inflation into stunning increases in wealth is not a theoretical discussion of the multiplication of the multiplication - it is instead the very real history of a nation, something that changed the lives of tens of millions of people. This is true even though what would turn out to be the best investment in their lives, was for many people more or less happenstance, and they never did fully understand what happened.

The aftermath of that time period is also the beginning of my personal experience with the subject matters of this book, and what helped to set me down the path to eventually researching and writing this book.

As a young investment banking vice president in the 1980s, I participated in the portfolio restructurings of billions of dollars of what were then known as "underwater" mortgage loans. For years, day after day, I spent my time analyzing portfolios from across the country. Whether the client was a small community savings & loan in Georgia or a multibillion dollar institution in Chicago, all of these financial institutions were carrying portfolios of hundreds, thousands, or even tens of thousands of little mortgages. With each of them bearing interest rates that seemed absurdly low by the standards of the 1980s.

By the mid to late 1980s, when a nice new home in the suburbs was already up to $100,000+ with then-current interest rates of 11%, 12% and 14%, there were all these little loans still outstanding of $4,000, $10,000, and $20,000 - and with interest rates of 7%, 8%, sometimes even 6% and below. Compared to even the home prices and mortgage rates of the 1980s, these were almost toy mortgages and toy mortgage payments.

Yet, the cumulative impact of these many millions of small low-interest rate mortgages were anything but small for my clients and the rest of the financial industry. Paying 10% and more to borrow money and having that money invested at 7% in mortgages, locked in annual losses on every one of those mortgages - which could quickly drive a savings and loan association into bankruptcy.

While not the subject of the numerous headlines and congressional hearings caused by the savings and loan mortgage debacle, something equally powerful was happening on the other side. This was that for every dollar of loss by the banks and savings and loans – there was a beneficiary, because of the unequal partnership.

The high rates of inflation that were destroying the value of the mortgages, were indeed stacking all the benefits of the Homeowner Wealth Formula up for many millions of people. Put in today's dollars, the wealth transfer from the financial industry to just average people throughout the country was in excess of $2 trillion.

The little guy was actually winning! (Even if it was a complete accident.) Every time my colleagues and I looked at a portfolio of a thousand "underwater" mortgages that was on the verge of bankrupting a $100 million financial institution, we were also looking at a thousand individual households who were enjoying the benefits of having bought a home with a mortgage and owning it during a time of high inflation.

We were looking at a thousand families who could recognize a fat profit anytime they sold their house, with their home equity growing at a rate that was well in excess of the rate of

The Homeowner Wealth Formula

inflation – because all the inflation gains had gone to them, and none to the mortgage lenders. Even better was when they didn't sell their home, and the inflation-driven shrinkage of the real cost of their mortgage payments freed up vast amounts of wealth (as covered in more detail in Book #3). These homeowners benefited every month they wrote one of those little mortgage payments that were bankrupting their lenders.

Indeed, while the primary database used herein starts in 1975 - a lot of inflation had already occurred by then. For people who bought homes in the 1960s or early 1970s, the results were on average much better for them, much more life changing, than what is shown in this chapter.

Without their even fully realizing the source of their good fortunes, wealth was given to these lucky people hand over fist, for year after year. Wealth that paid for new cars and new furniture. Wealth that paid for college tuition for children. Wealth that still forms the financial foundation for some older retirees today. This wealth in the form of home equity also formed the bulk of the estates that millions of people left to their children when they passed.

At the beginning of the 2020s many people fear that the exploding national debt could bring in another decade of high inflation at some point. If that were to happen, this is a good time to not have to rely upon accidental happenstance to survive such a time. The Homeowner Wealth Formula provides what may be the best single source of protection against inflation that is available to the average person, and hopefully this chapter has been helpful to the reader in understanding how that works.

Chapter 8

Strengthening The Natural Flow Of Wealth With Amortization

Amortization is the name for the process of steadily paying off a debt in increments. Every monthly mortgage payment consists of an interest component, and a principal component that pays off a portion of the loan. There are also often escrow payments for property taxes and home insurance as part of the monthly payment, but they aren't part of the mortgage payment itself. How much of each mortgage payment will go to paying down debt depends on the interest rate, type and remaining length of the mortgage.

There can be a lot of technical issues associated with mortgage amortization, but our focus in this book is the role of amortization in strengthening the natural flow of wealth that is the Homeowner Wealth Formula.

Three aspects of amortization are of particular importance to the overall wealth formula:

1) Amortization in general speeds up the rate at which equity is built, which increases the advantages to homeownership. *Indeed, there is a second level of stacking and multiplication, which stacks on top of the first level of stacking and multiplication of inflation gains that was explored in previous chapters.*

2) Amortization over time builds safety by materially reducing the chances of losses in equity. The longer that the one way process of inflation has time to work, the greater the safety margin, and the less the chances of losses in equity. Separately, the longer that the one way process of amortization has time to work, the greater the safety margin. When the two sources of safety margin are combined, this greatly increases the reliability of the Homeowner Wealth formula. Because each are independently getting much stronger with time, history shows us that the farther out in time that we go, the more powerful the combined safety margin has been in practice for homeowners.

3) There is a little understood but strong relationship between amortization speeds and rates of inflation at the time the mortgage is originated. This relationship is not random, but can create a natural hedge, where the weaker the benefits that are delivered by the inflation component of the Homeowner Wealth

Formula, the more powerful the benefits that are delivered by the amortization component. This natural self-protection further increases the size and reliability of the overall flow of wealth.

How Amortization Works & Where It Leads

If we look at a 30 year fixed rate mortgage and a homeowner making only their contractual payments - then the portion of the payment that goes to paying down the mortgage will be different for every one of the 360 monthly payments. Each mortgage payment reduces the remaining balance of the mortgage, the money that is still owed. Because the mortgage is smaller, this reduces the amount of interest that is due the following month, and that then increases the amount of money that goes to principal the next month.

	How A Mortgage Amortization Works			
	$150,000 Mortgage, 4% Interest Rate, 20 Years Remaining			
Month	Starting Mortgage	Monthly Payment	Monthly Interest	Monthly Principal
1	$150,000.00	$908.97	$500.00	$408.97
2	$149,591.03	$908.97	$498.64	$410.33
3	$149,180.70	$908.97	$497.27	$411.70
4	$148,768.99	$908.97	$495.90	$413.07
5	$148,355.92	$908.97	$494.52	$414.45
6	$147,941.47	$908.97	$493.14	$415.83
7	$147,525.64	$908.97	$491.75	$417.22
8	$147,108.42	$908.97	$490.36	$418.61
9	$146,689.81	$908.97	$488.97	$420.00

DanielAmerman.com

As an example, if we start with a $150,000, 4% loan with 240 payments remaining, the fixed monthly mortgage payments would be $908.97 (not including property taxes or home insurance). Of that, the interest payment for one month would be $500. This would leave $408.97 available to pay down the principal portion of the mortgage.

Because the mortgage has been very slightly paid down to $149,591, the second month of 4% interest on the remaining mortgage is slightly smaller as well, falling from $500 to $498.64. The payment is still fixed at $908.97, so that means that the amount of money available to pay down the mortgage slightly increases to $410.33. This is an increase of $1.36 in one month, and the mortgage after both payments is now down to $149,181.

In the third month, the 4% interest on the smaller mortgage is reduced again to $497.27, which leaves a slightly larger $411.70 payment to be applied to the principal, and so forth.

What starts small builds powerfully over the years. While beyond the scope of this book, the reason is that principal payments build with another variant of the compound interest formula. Because this is the case, the amortization speed exponentially compounds over time, growing much more powerful in ten or twenty years, but yet it is acutely sensitive to changes in mortgage interest rates.

What matters for homeowners is that because amortization depends on the actual interest rate, every time that we change the interest rate - we also change the amortization speed of the mortgage.

Now, some people might say that because we are paying the money to reduce the size of the mortgage, the resulting increase in home equity isn't really a gain - we had to pay for it.

The basic approach we are taking in this book is that we need a place to live, and for this first book, there is the assumption of at least a rough equivalence between rent and the sum of mortgage payments, property taxes, home insurance, and basic upkeep. The mortgage payments are effectively canceled out by not needing to make rent payments. This is much more the subject of Book #3 in this series, and in practice, history shows us that the monthly cash flow benefits of homeownership over time can equal or exceed the home equity benefits.

So, what we get in exchange for our mortgage payments is hopefully a very nice place to live our lives in, along with some rather extraordinary financial advantages that renters simply don't enjoy.

Net worth is equal to assets less debts. One side of the net worth equation that works strongly to the advantage of homeowners is the ability to increase assets, multiplying the benefits from inflation increasing the price of the home due to the unequal partnership with the mortgage lender.

The other equally valid side of increasing net worth and financial security is to reduce the amount of debts. Entering into a mortgage is entering into a mandatory debt reduction schedule - i.e., an amortization - where the debt is steadily paid down until it is extinguished. Many millions of households have indeed achieved this end destination that is available to homeowners but not renters, and now own the residence where they live free and clear. This creates tremendous advantages by substantially lowering monthly bills while increasing financial security.

The 2019 Federal Reserve *Survey of Consumer Finances* determined that about 35% of all homeowners own their primary residence outright, with no mortgage. If we take those many millions of households who did reach that destination, look at the $225,000 median home value in the U.S. - and compare that to the $65,000 median value of the retirement accounts for the 50% of households who have them - then a major discrepancy can be seen between the widespread theory of how we are supposed to create wealth, and the actual practice of how the nation has been doing it.

Start with a completely typical household, who can't pay cash for a place to live. Have them buy their house primarily with debt - but make them enter into a contract to pay that debt back each and every month, with those payments forming the core of their budget. Let them live their life in a nice place, perhaps while raising a family and with a dog in the back yard. The largest debt in their life is steadily paid down even while the value of their home is going through a doublings process over the decades that is primarily driven by inflation and the compound interest formula. Until the day comes where the debt is gone, the home is owned free and clear, and the market value of the home is far, far more than what was paid for it.

Some people would call this the American Dream, while others would not. Whatever one wants to call it - *we know it works.* We know that in practice for the typical family, the median household, this lived and shared American experience has eventually contributed far more to their net worth and financial security than savings in the bank, or stocks or bonds or mutual funds or ETFs.

An Abundance Of Amortizations

Long before that end destination is reached, however, amortization is steadily creating increases in home equity by decreasing the mortgage amount. In the example above of a $150,000 mortgage with a 4% mortgage and a 20 year remaining term - about 45% of the mortgage payments were initially going to paying down the debt, with over $3,000 being paid down in just the first nine months. That $3,000 reduction in debt goes straight to homeowner net worth and financial security - with no equivalent increase in net worth for renters.

Now, there are many other factors, such as having a 10, 15, or 30 year mortgage, or having a variable rate mortgage, or whether the homeowner sends in additional money to accelerate their mortgage. Some of those factors have the ability to materially speed up amortization, relative to what is shown in this chapter.

That said, sticking to our example of the very common thirty year, fixed rate, 80% LTV mortgage - we still have an abundance of amortizations. The amount of principal paid down in each month changes not only with the months of payments remaining, but also the interest rates on the mortgage. So, if we have two different mortgage interest rates, then we have two different amortizations - and the differences in how fast the mortgage pays down can be major.

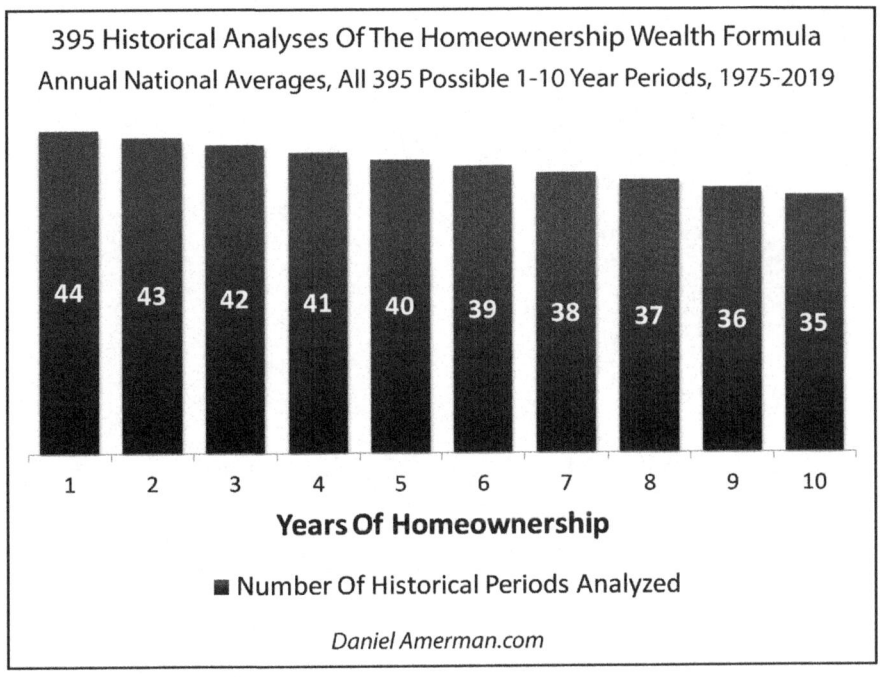

For this reason, in addition to looking at 395 different 1-10 year home price experiences between 1975 and 2019, and 395 different historical inflation rates, I also looked at 395 different amortizations. For each starting year, I took the national average thirty year mortgage rate for that year, ran an amortization, and then determined how much money was still owed after each of the first ten years of homeownership.

This added another level of complexity, but it was mandatory if we are to determine what the national average homeownership experience has been for the United States in each year, and to see just how the Homeownership Wealth Formula has worked in practice for all those tens of millions of households.

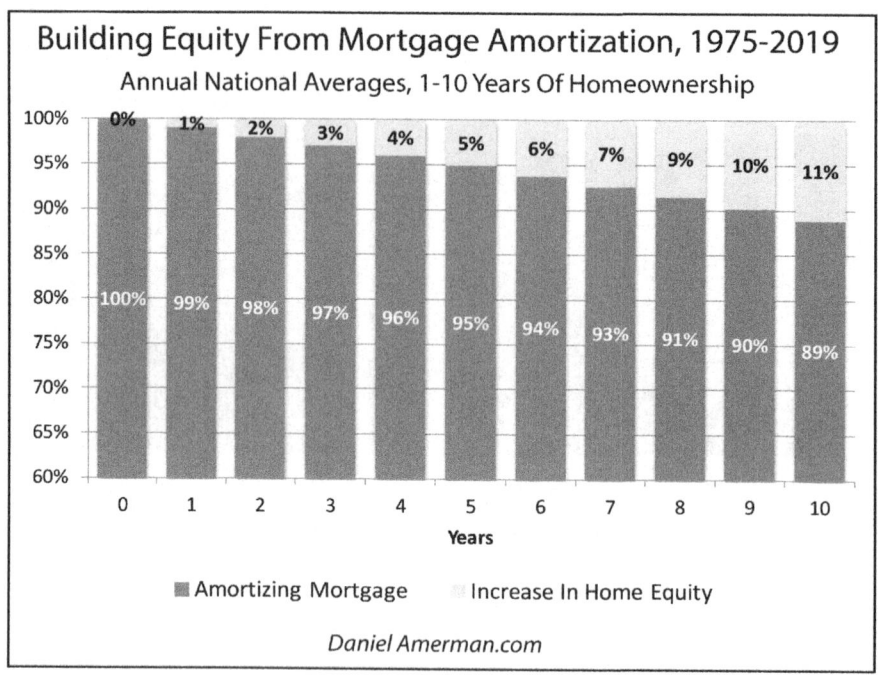

The national average results based upon all 395 possibilities are shown in the graph above. On average about 1% of the mortgage balance was paid down in the first year. The average was that about 5% of the mortgage was paid down in five years, and about 11% in ten years. This means that about 95% of the mortgage was still outstanding after five years, and 89% of the mortgage was still owed when we go ten years out.

If we look at the resulting size of the increase in home equity, and the reliability of the increase in home equity, then this is much easier if we compare the amortization to just the home equity instead of the overall home price.

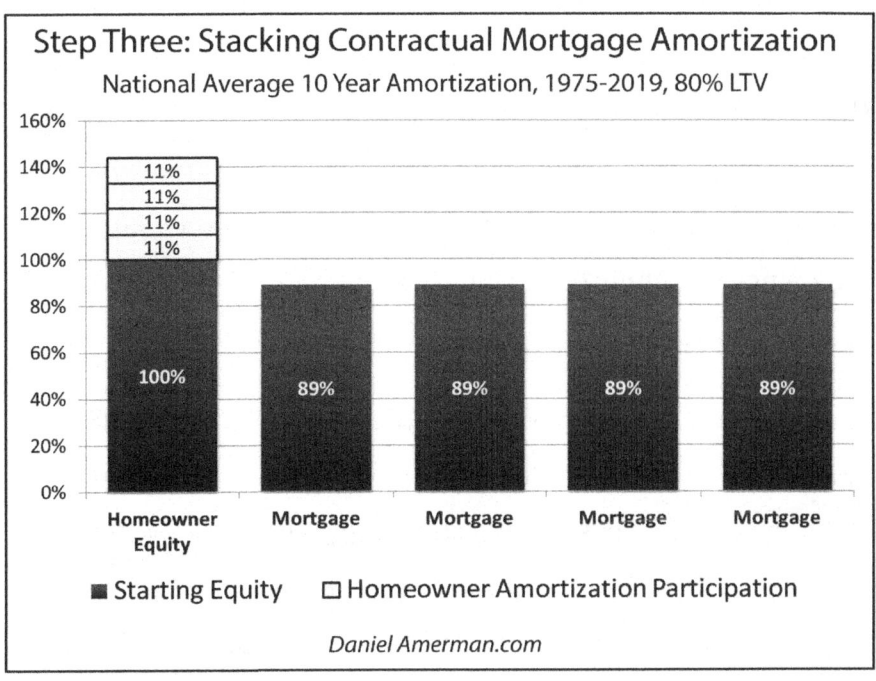

The graph above shows amortization relative to starting equity and it also returns to the stacking concept, although in a different form than with inflation gains. As before, with an 80% LTV mortgage we start off with 5 equal buckets, with the homeowner funding 20%, and the lender funding four matching equal buckets of 20% each.

After ten years, on average each of the four mortgage buckets would be down to 89% still outstanding. However, there is no amortization for the 20% starting home equity. For a $200,000 home with a $160,000 mortgage - there are only four $40,000 mortgage buckets to be reduced. Therefore the buckets are only stacked four high with amortization, instead of the five high for inflation gains.

All four 11% amortizations go to the benefit of the homeowner, and they stack on top of the homeowner equity. This means that looking at all 35 possible ten year homeownership periods, and at national average mortgage interest rates in the year of home purchase for each possibility, the average homeowner saw their home equity increase by 44% solely as a result of contractual mortgage amortization.

Returning to the $200,000 home example, there is no amortization of the $40,000 equity bucket. Each of the four $40,000 mortgage buckets are reduced by 11%, or $4,400, as the result of a portion of each monthly mortgage payment going to paying down principal. Home equity is the value of the home, minus the remaining mortgage, so decreases in debt go straight into homeowner equity. Stacking the four $4,400 increases in equity on top is a $17,600 increase in equity. A $17,600 increase in equity is equal to 44% of the starting $40,000.

An alternative conceptual path to the same destination is to just reduce the mortgage by 11%, from $160,000 down to $142,400. Take a $200,000 home with no price gains, subtract a $142,400 mortgage, and the home equity is $57,600. This $17,600 increase in equity from amortization alone is equal to 44% of the starting $40,000.

This is the fourth level of the multiplication of wealth - the multiplication and four high stacking that occurs with amortization increases in equity when a home is purchased with a mortgage.

High Interest Rates & Slow Amortizations

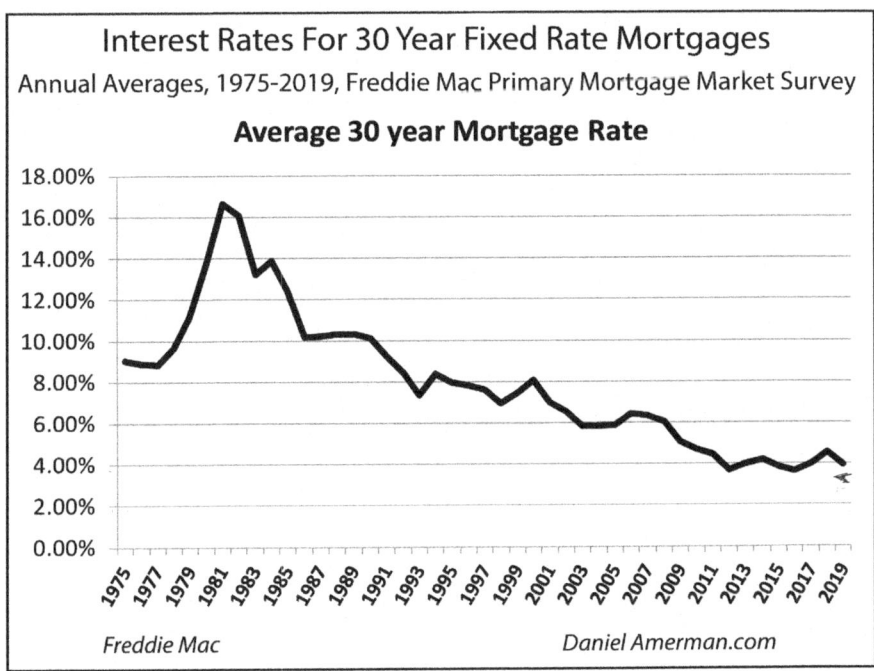

The graph above shows annual average mortgage interest rates between 1975 and 2019 - and there is a great deal of variation. The peak was in 1981, at a 16.63% national average mortgage rate. The lowest average rate (prior to 2020) was 3.65%

in 2016. The lowest rate for which we have a full ten years of home price data is the 5.04% national average rate for 2009.

Those changes in mortgage rates matter greatly because the higher the mortgage rate, then the slower the amortization. Conversely, the lower the mortgage rate, then the faster the amortization - and the difference for homeowner equity in the early years can be quite material.

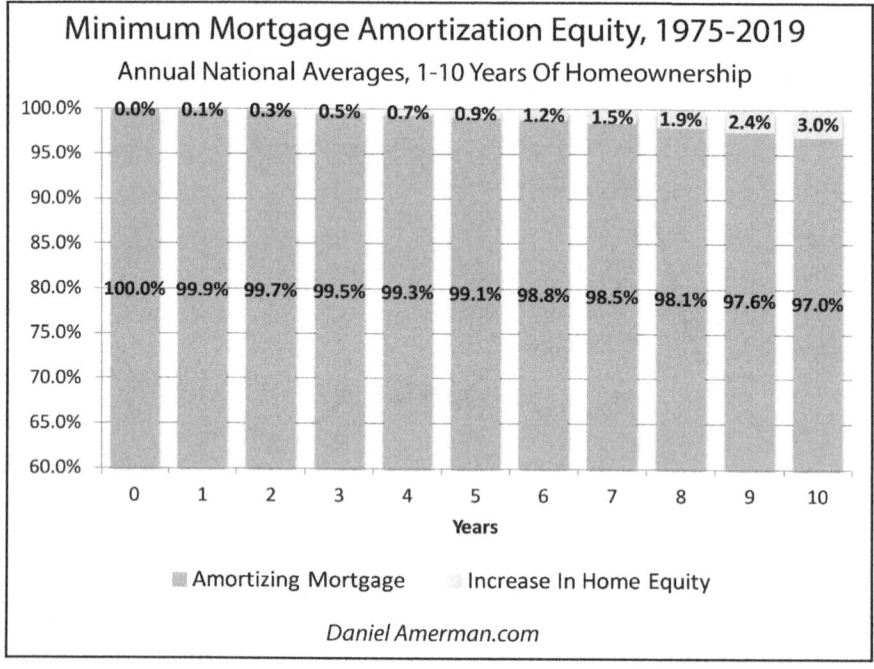

Because the peak annual mortgage rate occurred in 1981, homeowners who bought in 1981 had the slowest amortizations out of all the possibilities.

It took six years to reduce the mortgage by an amount equal to 0.9%, instead of the one year with the average of the amortizations. Only 3% was paid off over ten years, instead of the 11% with the average of the amortizations.

So just how bad was it for the homeowner if they get stuck with a very slow amortization?

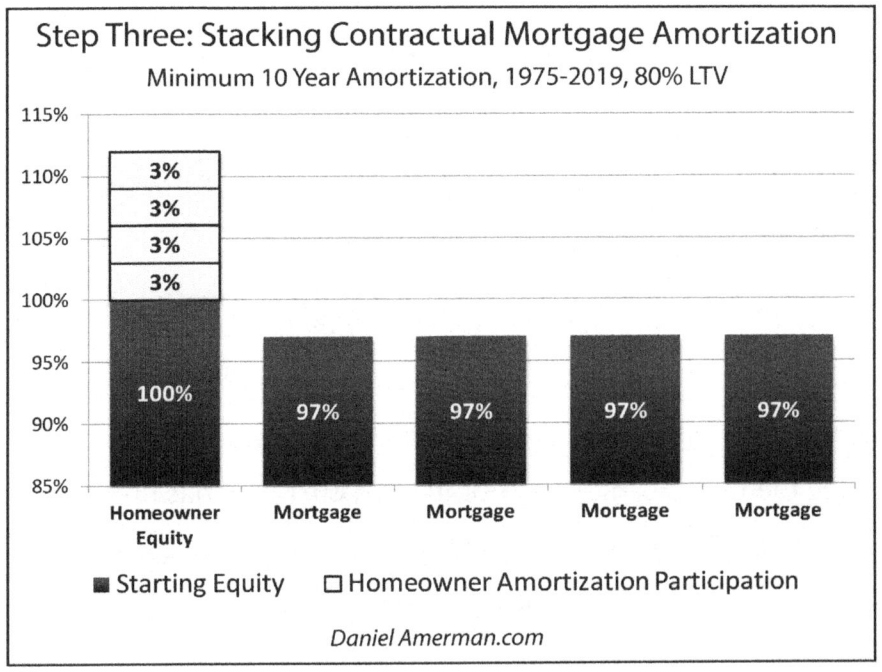

The above is our stacking and multiplication graph for the worst ten years for mortgage amortizations, which was for homes purchased in 1981.

Again, there is no amortization for the equity bucket, but there is a 3% amortization for each of the four mortgage buckets, so we multiply times four, and stack all four on top of the equity bucket. The worst historical case is a 12% increase in home equity over 10 years from mortgage amortization alone.

The amounts are small enough where we had to zoom in on the vertical scale, or the 3% increments would have been hard to see on the graph.

But, nonetheless, they are there, they are positive, and they are multiplied times four to determine the increase in homeowner equity.

There are similarities when it comes to minimum inflation gains and minimum increases in equity resulting from mortgage amortization.

With inflation, the primary source of the gains is not rolling the dice or speculating on the market - but government policy. The highly reliable track record of the government seeking to reduce the purchasing power of its own currency has created inflation in 394 out of the 395 possibilities. Every single one of the 394 positive outcomes is then multiplied times five with an 80% LTV mortgage.

With amortization, the source of the increase in equity is not based on the markets but is instead contractual, it is set when the mortgage is closed. This means it produces increases in equity 395 out of 395 times - and each of those increases is multiplied times four with an 80% LTV mortgage, when we are calculating the impact on homeowner equity.

The two highly reliable sources work together in combination, reinforcing each other when it comes to the size of the increase in home equity, and reinforcing each other when it comes to safety and reliably building financial security over time.

It is also worth noting that a big part of the reason for a financially educated investor to own investment real estate, is to use the renter's money (in the form of rent payments) to make the mortgage payments to access the 394 out of 395 inflation gains AND to get the 395 out of 395 amortization benefits. Both are happening regardless of whether a home is owned or rented (assuming the landlord used a mortgage to buy the property, as most do). The question is who gets the benefits - and they go to the property owner either way, homeowner or investor, but never to the renter.

Low Interest Rates & Fast Amortizations

Low interest rates produce much faster amortization speeds.

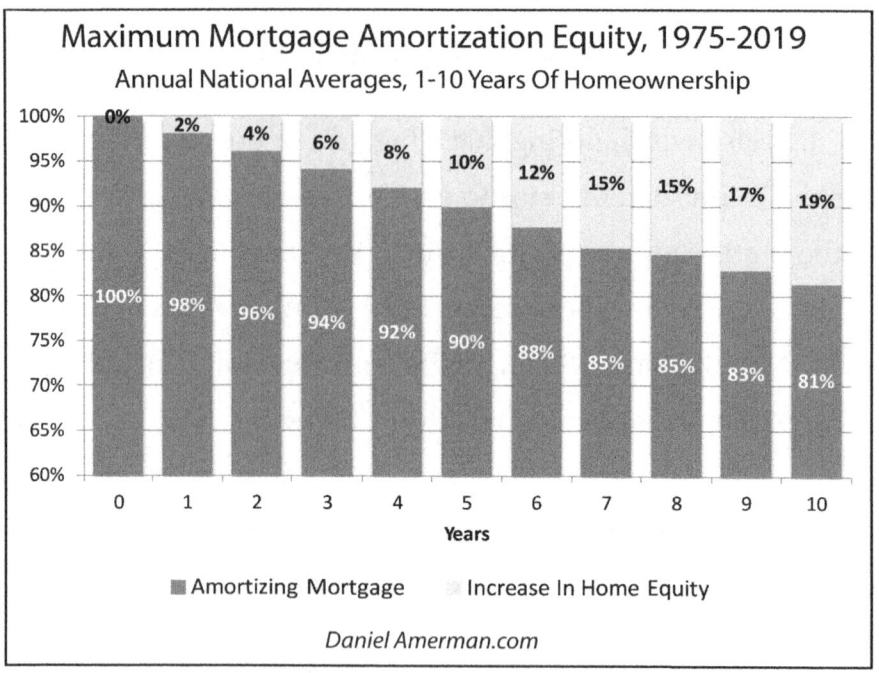

To get the fastest amortization we need to find the lowest mortgage rates. If we look at all 40 of the five year homeownership periods, the lowest mortgage rate that we have five years of inflation and home price data on is the 3.66% rate for homes purchased in 2012. The national average for homes purchased in 2012 was to pay down 10% of the mortgage in just five years, which is twice the average result, and *11 times faster than the slowest five year amortization of 0.9%*.

As of the writing of this book we don't have ten years of data on homes purchased in 2012. The lowest mortgage rate for which ten years of home information is available is the national average mortgage rate of 5.04% for 2009. Over ten years, that 5.04% rate produced the fastest mortgage amortization of 19% of the starting mortgage amount. *This is about 73% faster than the average amortization, and about 6 times faster than the slowest amortization.* Interest rates matter for amortization, and they matter greatly.

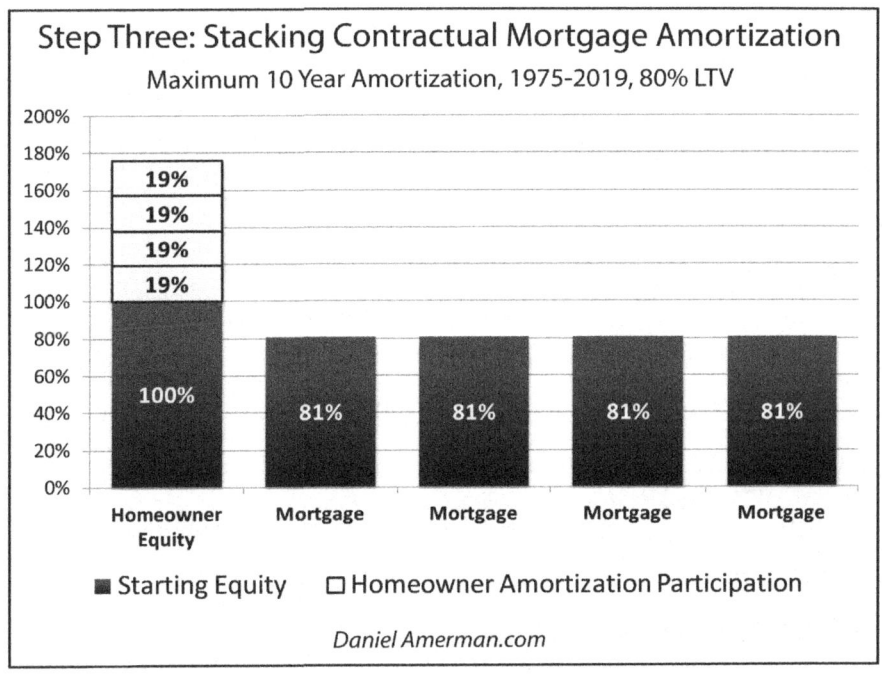

The stacking graph above shows the impact on home equity of the fastest ten year amortization for the nation, that of the 2009-2019 period.

Each of the four mortgage buckets would have gone down to 81% by 2019. All four of the resulting 19% (rounded) increases in home equity would then stack on top of the homeowner equity bucket. Multiplying times four, amortization alone would account for a 76% increase in homeowner equity over the period of ten years.

If we compare the gains from amortization only, then out of all 35 of the ten year possibilities, the national average was a 44% increase in equity. The lowest increase in equity was 12%. The highest increase in equity was 76%, which was six times greater than the lowest increase.

Looking Ahead With Contractual Amortizations

Mortgage amortization speeds are a matter of contract, and the debt repayment schedule is fixed at the time the mortgage is closed. So, we don't know what inflation will be over the next five years, ten years or twenty years. We don't know what changes in real market value will be for the nation over those years. But, as of the time that a mortgage closes at a given interest rate - we do know what the minimum amortization schedule will be (homeowners do have the option of accelerating the pay down of their mortgage by sending extra money in early).

As a very relevant example, thirty year mortgage rates moved below 3% in 2020. As a matter of contract, a 3% mortgage will be reduced by 11% over the first five years. For someone who closes on a 3% mortgage as part of purchasing their home, they know in advance that their increase in equity in the first five years will be more than twice the historic average of 5%. At the time of closing, the homeowner knows that they have no risk of the minimum five year amortization of 0.9%, and they know that they have instead locked in a mortgage that will amortize a full twelve times as fast as that minimum.

A 3% mortgage will pay down 24% of the principal amount over the first ten years, and this is known at the time of the home and mortgage closing.

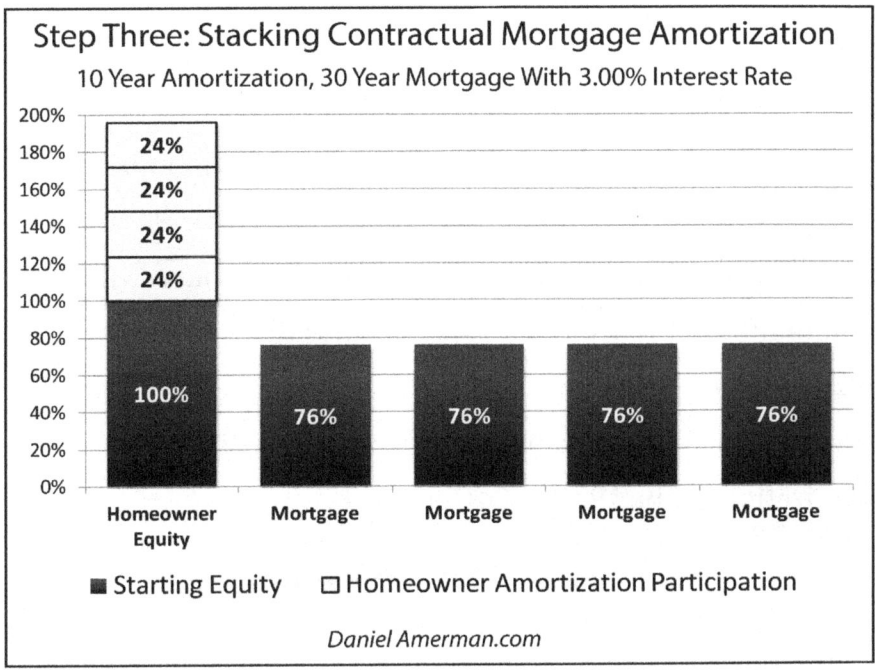

This means that there is a 24% increase in home equity as a result of amortization for each one of the four mortgage buckets. When we stack those 4 amortization increases in equity on top of the starting home equity - we get a 96% increase in home equity over ten years.

For a $200,000 home with one $40,000 home equity bucket, and four $40,000 mortgage buckets - there is no amortization gain for the home equity bucket itself. But, the four mortgage buckets are reduced by $9,600 each as a result of amortization. When those $9,600 increases in equity are stacked four high on top of starting home equity, then home equity increases by $38,400 to $78,400, or almost double the starting equity, solely from contractual amortization.

For those homeowners who are able to close on homes financed by these very low interest rate mortgages - this gives them an assurance of an outcome from amortization that exceeds anything we can see in the historical record. With a 3% mortgage, just sending in the lower payments each month that are the result of the very low interest rate, has the advantageous side effect of locking in an almost doubling of home equity in the first ten years, which is better than anything seen with ten years of amortization in the 1975 to 2019 period.

When added to normal inflation and real market value changes, that by itself pushes expected gains in home equity well above the historic norm. Because it is a matter of contract, this large built-in amortization advantage can also be very forgiving when it comes to overcoming low rates of inflation, as well as adverse changes in real market values for homes.

It should also be noted that if inflation rates rise after the mortgage closes - that does not change the interest rate on a fixed rate mortgage. So, if someone were to buy a home using a very low fixed rate mortgage, and the nation was to subsequently

The Homeowner Wealth Formula

experience rising inflation rates over the years that followed, *that would create an ideal mathematical combination for rapidly increasing homeowner wealth.* The simultaneous rapid increase in the price of the asset, in combination with the record speed of reducing the debt - with each then being stacked five or four high - would create a fast growing differential that could build homeowner net worth at a potentially record pace.

Chapter 9

The Homeowner Wealth Formula & The Nine High Stack

To see the underlying core of the full Homeowner Wealth Formula, we have to combine the first four levels of the multiplication of wealth:

1) we start with the annual rates of inflation;

2) we compound that inflation using the power of the compound interest formula;

3) we stack the compounded inflation gains five high because of the unequal partnership, and

4) we then stack the amortization increases in equity four high.

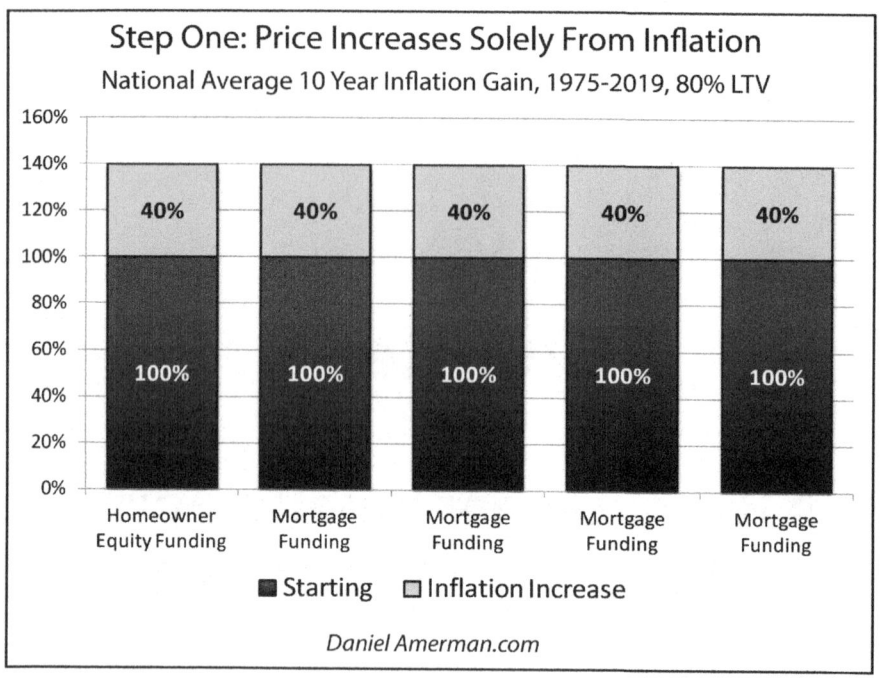

Looking at all possible ten year periods between 1975 and 2019, the national average experience was to see inflation by itself increase the prices of everything - including homes - by an average of 40%.

The Homeowner Wealth Formula

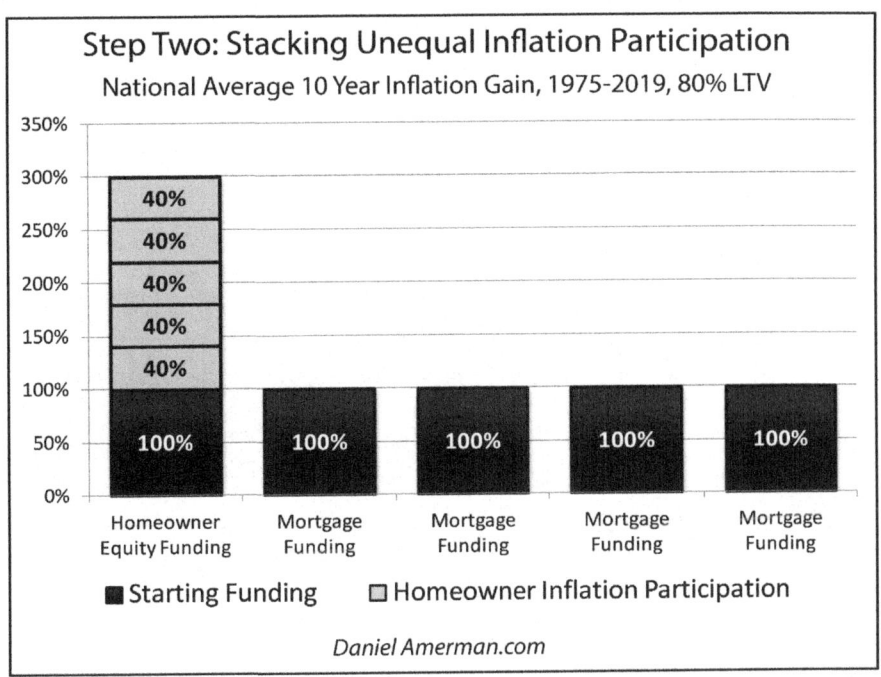

Because of the unequal partnership between the homeowner and mortgage lender, all of the inflation gains from all five buckets (with an 80% LTV mortgage) go to homeowners where they stack on top of each other.

In other words, the national average experience over the decades was to see inflation by itself created a wealth driver that was sufficient to triple homeowner equity in ten years.

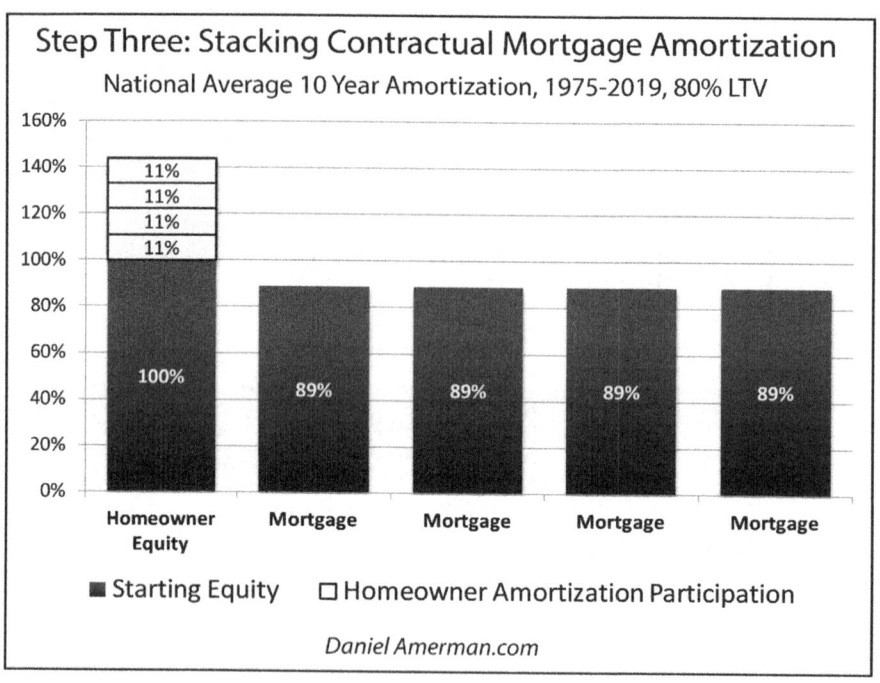

Separately if we look at all 35 possible national average mortgage rates in each starting year, and calculate how much amortization would occur over the following ten years with each of those rates - the average was that 11% of the mortgage would be paid down.

There is no amortization of the starting equity bucket, but all four of the amortizations from the mortgage buckets go directly to increasing the net worth of the homeowner. Stacking those four on top of each other, the average national experience for the many millions of households over the decades was to see their home equity increase by 44% in ten years, solely as a result of mortgage amortization.

The Homeowner Wealth Formula 179

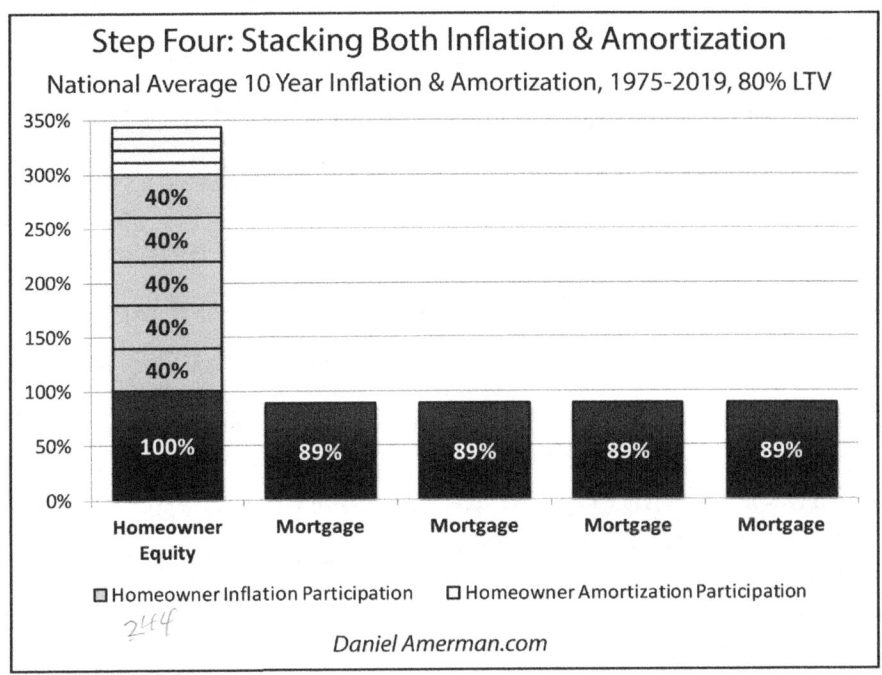

Daniel Amerman.com

When we stack the five 40% inflation gains on top of each other, and then stack the four 11% amortization increases in equity on top of those, we get the how the core of how the Homeowner Wealth Formula has worked in practice for the United States as a whole since 1975.

For all of those millions of households, across all those years of buying homes - *the national average result was to have a natural flow of wealth created that would increase their home equity by about 3.43 times in the first ten years of home ownership.*

For a $200,000 home purchased with $40,000 in equity, the national average was to see an almost $100,000 gain in the first ten years, with home equity increasing to $137,000 just from the first four levels of the multiplication of wealth.

For anyone reading this who owned a home or homes over those decades - it is unlikely that all of your personal experience is entirely explained by this, but it is quite likely that most of your personal experience can be explained by these factors.

This is still not everything - but what we have covered in this first book is most of everything, and it is overwhelmingly positive.

On average, for the nation and over the years, the great majority of homeowner wealth gains are not about luck and they aren't about skill. Most wealth gains have not been driven by the skill of picking the right neighborhood to buy in (although skill can certainly help), nor are they about the luck of the particular year in which someone purchased their home.

For the nationally average homeowner, what has dominated their personal financial experience with homeownership has simply been positioning for themselves to benefit from the natural flow of wealth.

To position themselves so that government policies of steadily destroying the value of the dollar naturally create inflation gains that stack five high on top of each other. To choose to make mortgage payments instead of rental payments for their place of residence, and to then have another four layers of amortization gains naturally stack on top of the five layers of inflation gains. This creates a nine high stack of home equity increases for them.

Equity Gains That Build Fast

Crucially, homeowners have not needed to wait ten years for the benefits from amortization to be quite useful.

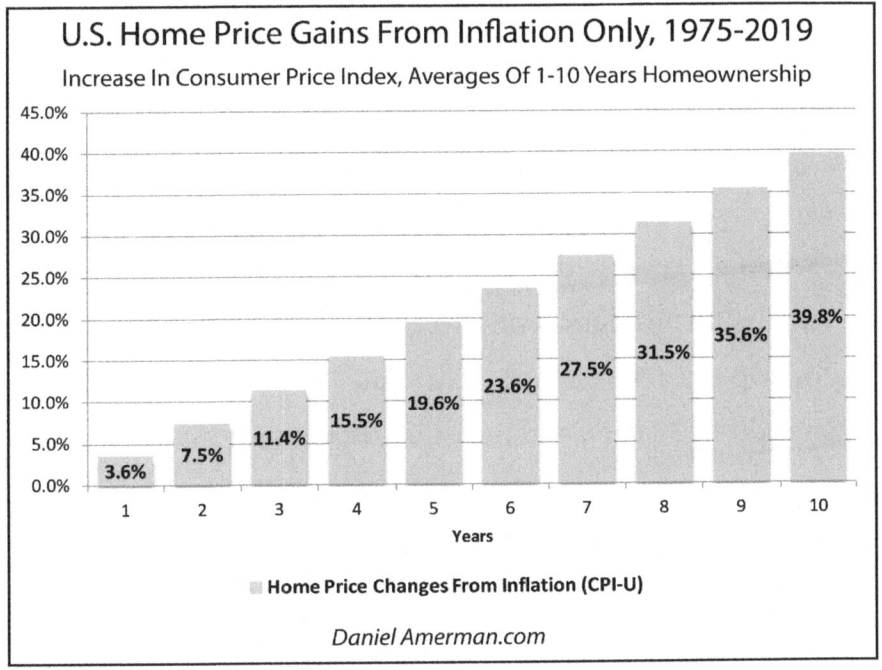

Average gains from inflation - which is again usually a wealth destroyer for most people - means that it takes on average

11% more money to buy things in 3 years, and 27% more in 7 years.

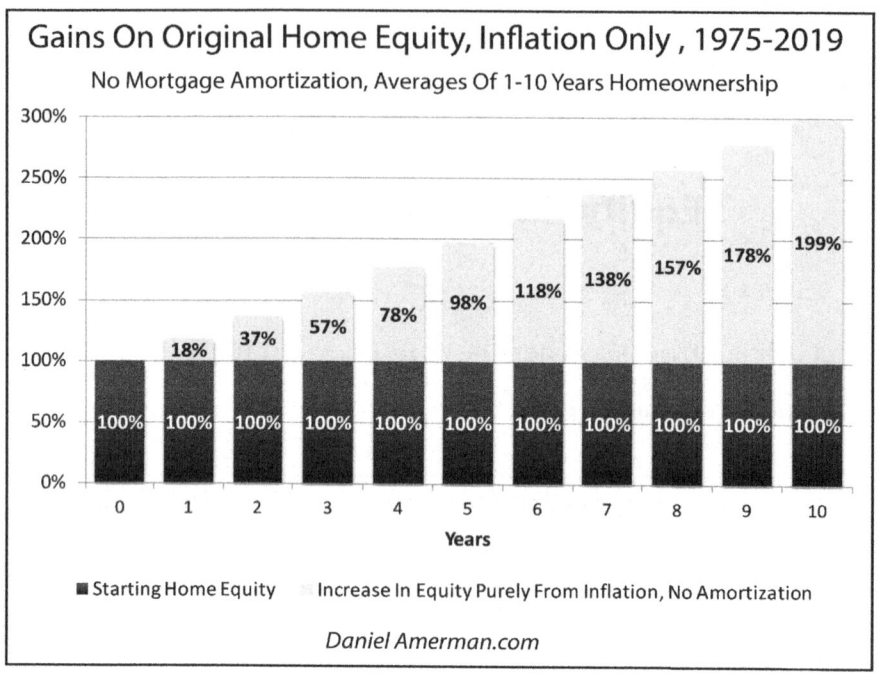

When we reverse the flow with the mortgage and unequal partnership, turn inflation into wealth, and stack the five inflation gains on top of each year - that translates to a 57% national average gain in 3 years, and over the decades, a 138% gain in 7 years. So 1.6 times the starting equity in only 3 years, and about 2.4 times the money in just 7 years.

The Homeowner Wealth Formula

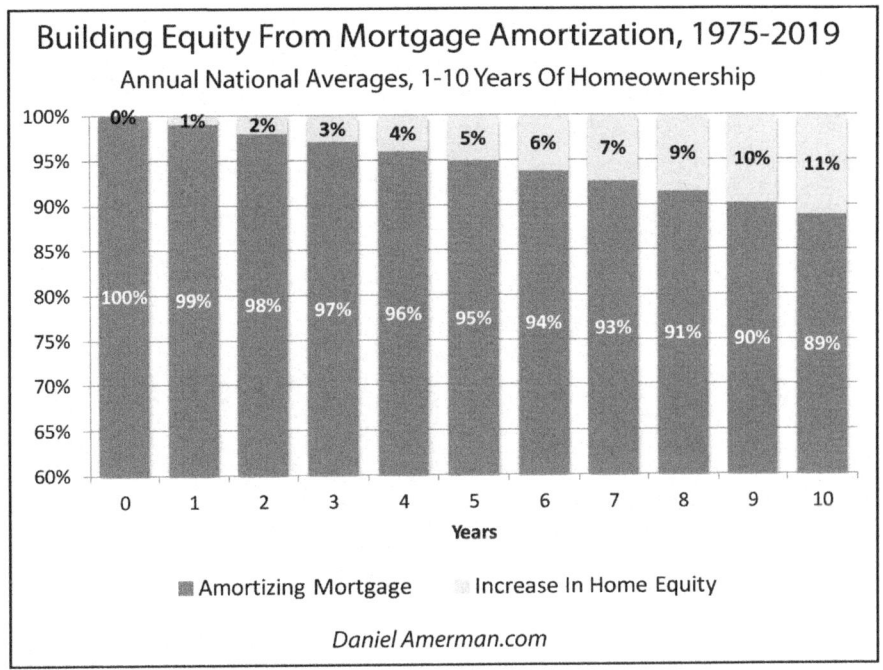

The early year mortgage amortizations are not overwhelming - but they do help.

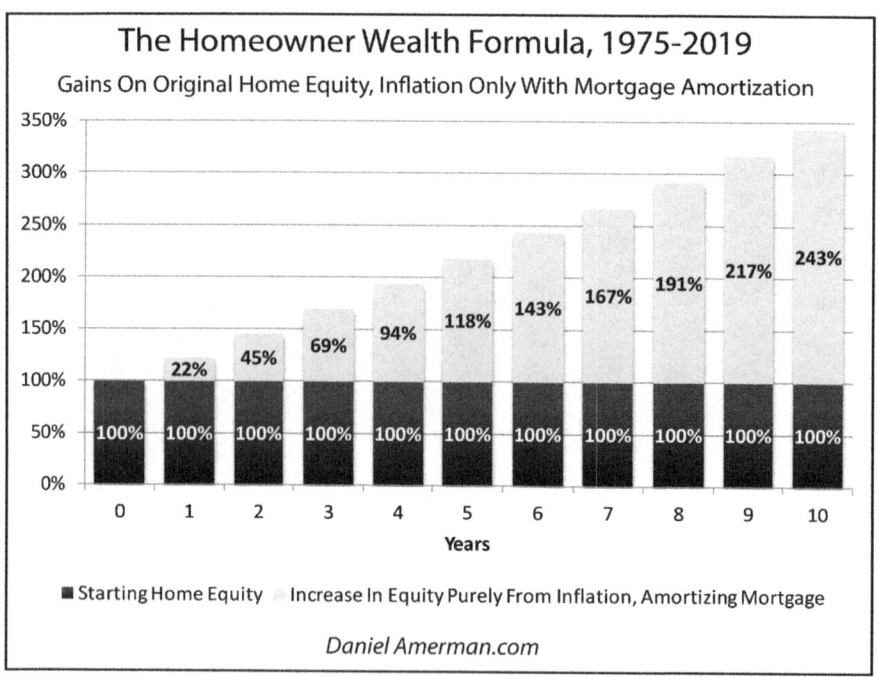

When we combine the five inflation gains with the four amortization increases in equity, then we go to a 1.7 times increase in equity in only 3 years.

When we give both inflation and amortization more time to follow their cumulative and one way paths, then the natural result for the nation as a whole has been to see just those two factors increase home equity by 2.7 times over 7 years - which is becoming very useful and material indeed.

Moving From 99.7% To 100% Wealth Drivers Safety

As can be seen above, amortization is not as powerful of force as inflation has been over the years - but it is cumulative on top of inflation, and it increases reliability. This increase in reliability can be seen when we look at the 1 time out of 395 possibilities that inflation failed to deliver, which was the 2008 to 2009 one year home ownership period.

This single worst case was an inflation gain of negative 0.3%, which is also referred to as deflation.

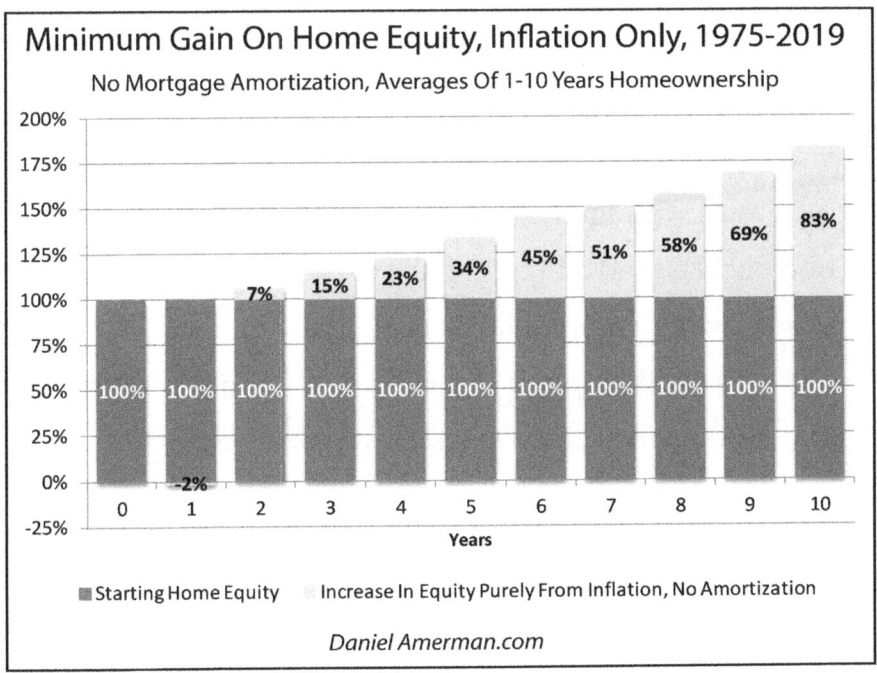

Homeowners would have experienced this loss with all five buckets. It would therefore have been multiplied times five, for a 1.5% loss on starting home equity, in what would seem to be a classic case of the costs of leverage (rounded to -2% in the graph above).

However, there was an offset. The national average 30 year mortgage rate in 2008 was 6.04%. If we calculate a mortgage amortization schedule, that means that there would have been a contractual 1.2% reduction in the mortgage amount by the end of the first year. Now, that amount is less than the loss from inflation - but this is where the four buckets come in.

With four mortgage buckets in an 80% LTV mortgage, we multiply four times 1.2% which is a 4.8% increase in equity. *The 4.8% increase in equity from amortization exceeded the 1.5% decrease from inflation, and flipped the negative to a positive.* When we start with the 1.5% inflation-related loss from the five inflation buckets, and add on top the 4.8% increase in equity from the four amortization buckets, then the national average homeowner would have experienced a 3.3% gain from those two wealth drivers in their first year of homeownership.

The Homeowner Wealth Formula

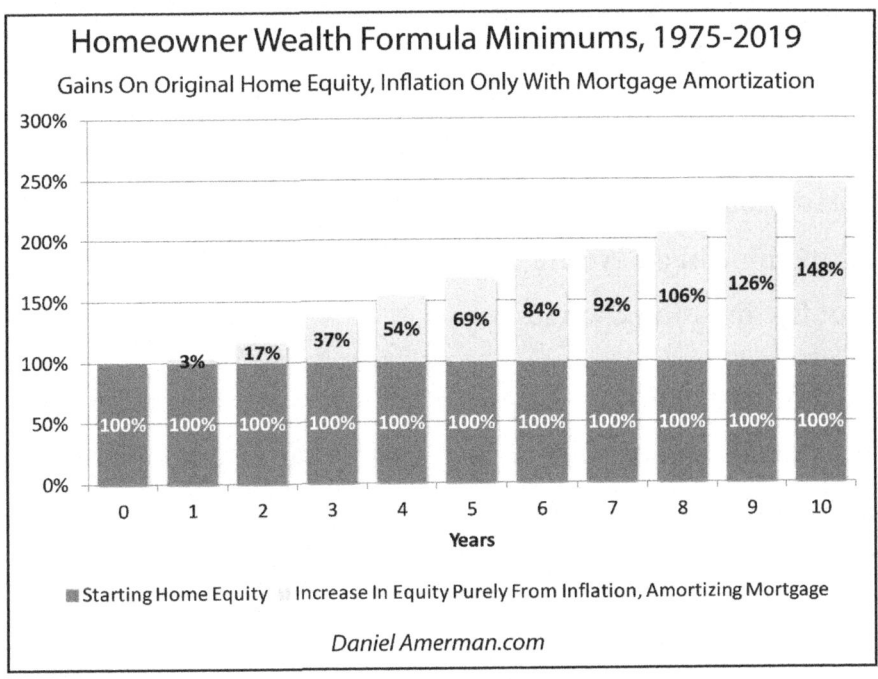

The minimums from every one of the Homeowner Wealth Formula possibilities are now positive. With all 395 of the 1-10 year possibilities between 1975 and 2019, the combination of inflation gains and mortgage amortization produced positive results all 395 times, for a 100% success rate.

Stacking Nine High With 100% Confidence

When we combine inflation gains and mortgage amortizations within an 80% LTV mortgage - then we are stacking nine high. We are stacking four amortization changes on top of five inflation changes.

For anyone who is familiar with leverage in the usual sense, our palms should be starting to get sweaty just thinking about the degree of risk that is associated with stacking nine high.

With normal leverage, this would be like taking our entire stack of chips in a casino and betting the whole thing on one spin of the roulette wheel. For poker, this should be like betting everything we have on our ability to draw into an inside straight. For someone used to investing in the markets, this should be analogous to taking our entire life savings, and using all the money to make one bet on buying deep out-of-the-money call options.

Stacking nine high should be terrifying. Any person or couple thinking of buying a home should be sweating bullets at the prospect. If this were ordinary leverage - then any rational home buyer's hands should be trembling when they sign the mortgage, sue to the prospect of imminent doom, multiplied nine times over.

But, that has not been the average homebuyer experience at all. When looking at homes, people have been free to look at things like school districts, walk-in closets and kitchens, instead of thinking about seemingly abstract financial matters like stacking nine high.

Mathematically, the nine high stack is leverage. If the stacks were ordinary leverage, then the risks would be acute. The reason that the risks are not acute is that the nine high stacks aren't based on the markets, randomness, gambling or speculation.

The stacking of the five high inflation gains is based on an alignment with government policies for reducing the value of the dollar that have been successful 394 out of 395 times. The stacking of the four amortization increases in equity is based on the mortgage contracts. Because it is a contractual feature rather than based on the markets, it has (of course) been successful 395 out of 395 times.

To have a nine high stack that in combination delivered positive results in all 395 possible 1-10 year ownership periods, for a success rate of 100% is amazing. This should be so improbable that it would be fantastic for something like that to happen. But, yet that is the shared homeowner experience for the many tens of millions of households over the decades from 1975 through 2019.

What makes this extraordinary, improbable nine times stacking of home equity increases even more fascinating - is that it came as more or less of a complete accident for the great majority of the people who have benefited from it.

This means that the combination of home prices rising with inflation, in an unequal partnership, where the partnership terms naturally change over time with the amortization of the mortgage - is a genuine and very powerful natural flow of wealth. What should take great skill, or great luck in terms of pulling off the nine high stack, is instead the almost certain outcome of just being in the right position for the benefits to flow to oneself.

This 99.7% or 100% reliability is not everything. There are still ways for homeowners to lose money. For instance, while amortization did overcome negative inflation results in the 2008 to 2009 period, homeowners did in fact lose money on average and quite a bit of it.

The Homeowner Wealth Formula

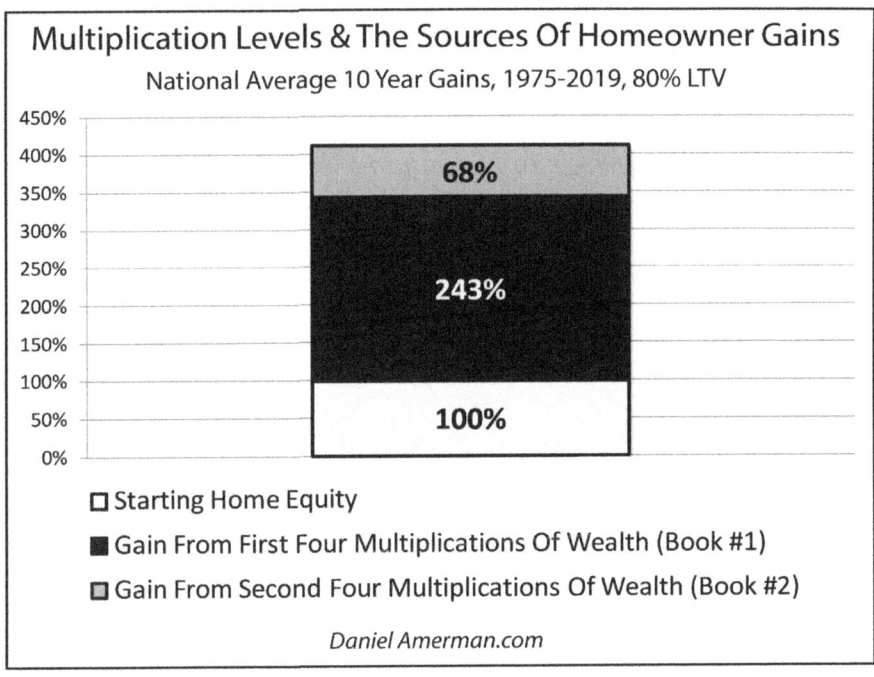

What we explored in this book are the underlying wealth drivers for homeownership. The non-market fundamentals that we examined do account for 3.43X out of the 4.11X national average increase in home equity over ten years. These powerful wealth drivers not only produced most of the increase in wealth for homeowners, but even more of the reliability of that increase in wealth. This has fundamentally shifted the odds in favor of homeowners, in ways that are simply not available in casinos - or generally in the markets either.

The remaining 0.68X average increase in homeowner equity over ten years is the result of the second four levels of the multiplication of wealth. These levels add a wild card - genuine changes in inflation-adjusted home market values, and how those interact with inflation and mortgages. A chapter and topic outline for Book #2 in this series can be found in the next section.

Book #2 Chapter Overview

The Eight Levels Of Homeowner Wealth Multiplication

(Expected publication in early 2021, book & chapter titles are subject to change.)

Chapter 1: Home Price Changes That Are Not From Inflation

Seeing real (inflation-adjusted) gains in market value

Seeing real (inflation-adjusted) losses in market value

The fifth level of the multiplication of wealth

Changes in the housing market since 2000

Average real home price changes over 1-10 year periods

The historical chances of real market value gains versus losses

Chapter 2: The Obscure But Powerful Seventh Level Of The Multiplication Of Wealth

The multiplication of real gains and inflation

The seventh level of the multiplication of wealth

The annual multiplications

Chapter 3: The History Of Eight Levels Of The Multiplication Of Wealth

The sixth level of the multiplication of wealth

The eighth level of the multiplication of wealth

Putting all eight levels together for homeowners over the long term

Comparing just the seventh and eighth levels to median retirement accounts

Chapter 4: Mapping Out The 19 Sources Of Long Term Homeowner Gains

Creating a visual wealth map for the average homeownership experience

The nineteen sources over the long term

The Homeowner Wealth Formula

Mapping real market value gains

Visualizing the combined effects of the first through eighth levels of wealth multiplication

Chapter 5: Rapid Wealth Creation From Nineteen Sources

Wealth map of 19 sources of almost doubling average home equity in three years

Wealth map of 19 sources of tripling average home equity in seven years

Wealth map of 19 sources of quadrupling average home equity in ten years

Chapter 6: Falling Real Home Prices & Using The Formula To Reduce Risk By 80%

Focusing on the worst case national average homeownership experiences

The real estate bubble, the financial crisis & the "worst of the worst"

The multiplication of the worst

How inflation reduces the risk of home equity losses by 72%

How inflation & amortization reduce the likelihood of losses by 80%

How inflation & amortization changed the "worst of the worst"

Historical years of homeownership needed to completely offset market risk

Chapter 7: Getting Lucky & The 23% Chance Of Getting The Price Of A House For Free

What happened when homeowners were lucky instead of unlucky

The best case national average homeownership experiences

The two types of homeowner "lottery tickets" and their multiplication

Wealth map of peak 3 year gains

Wealth map of peak 6 year gains

Wealth maps of all eight times national average homeowners "won the lottery"

Chapter 8: The National Debt & Future Wealth Maps

The relationship between inflation and large national debts

How governments use higher rates of inflation to control large national debts

How large national debts penalize savers while benefitting homeowners

Future wealth map of home equity gains with 3% inflation

Future wealth map of home equity gains with 6% inflation

Future wealth map of home equity gains with 9% inflation

Chapter 9: Population Growth & Future Wealth Maps

Population growth & other sources of real market value increases

The potential explosive increase in home equity from the multiplication of population growth and higher inflation from soaring national debts

The eight levels of the multiplication of wealth with population growth and 3% inflation

The eight levels of the multiplication of wealth with population growth and 6% inflation

The eight levels of the multiplication of wealth with population growth and 9% inflation

Other Financial Education Resources

(Available at DanielAmerman.com)

Free Course

Free 20+ chapter online course on the investment implications of cycles of crisis and the containment of crisis for stocks, bonds, real estate and precious metals

Workshops

(check website for more information)

Video Courses

Creating Win-Win-Win Solutions Using Real Estate-Based Asset/Liability Management Strategies

(This is the more sophisticated Turning Inflation Into Wealth course for real estate investors, rather than homeowners.)

Gold Out Of The Box, 2020s Edition

(A different intensive study of 50 years of financial history, this time it is devoted to better understanding secular cycles for gold, and finding superior investment & hedging strategies.)

Investment Strategies For Crisis & The Containment Of Crisis

Author Information

Daniel R. Amerman is a Chartered Financial Analyst and finance MBA with over 30 years of professional financial experience. He is the creator of a number of books and video courses on finance and economics. Articles by Mr. Amerman or referencing his work have appeared in numerous publications and websites, including Reuters, MarketWatch, U.S. News & World Report, MSN Money, Seeking Alpha, Business Insider, ValueWatch, Nasdaq.com, Morningstar.com, TalkMarkets and Financial Sense.

As an investment banking vice president in the 1980s, Mr. Amerman began working with real estate investors and developers in structuring optimum financings for real estate investments. These multimillion dollar deals involved using mortgages and reserves to obtain investment grade ratings on bonds that were issued to fund the acquisition or construction of multifamily residences (apartment buildings), portfolios of multifamily residences, assisted care facilities and nursing homes.

Mr. Amerman also did groundbreaking work as an investment banker and wholesale mortgage banker in the such areas as CMO/REMIC originations as part of portfolio restructurings for financial institutions. This involved working with numerous savings & loan associations in the aftermath of the inflationary crisis of the 1970s and 1980s, and their portfolios of thousands of small and low interest rate mortgages.

It was that combination of working as an expert with sophisticated real estate investment strategies, while also seeing the enormously positive financial impact of what average people were experiencing in small towns and cities all across the nation as the more or less accidental result of having bought homes with mortgages during a time of turmoil and inflation, that would eventually lead to The Homeowner Wealth Formula book and series.

In the 1990s, Mr. Amerman worked as an independent quantitative analyst, providing expert structural, analytical and mathematical verification services for the trust departments of major banks, investment banks, and rating agencies, mostly in real estate and mortgage related areas. During those same years Mr. Amerman wrote his first two books on investment and security analysis for institutional investors, that were published by McGraw-Hill (and subsidiary): *Mortgage Securities*, and

Collateralized Mortgage Obligations: Unlock The Secrets Of Mortgage Derivatives.

Many of the highly sophisticated strategies used by institutional investors, major banks and hedge funds for real estate and mortgage investment were almost completely unknown by average individual investors, they were of a fundamentally different nature than the usual personal finance and investment strategies. Mr. Amerman decided to focus on developing and teaching simpler and understandable strategies for individuals, that were also of a fundamentally different nature than the usual consumer financial education. This led to the original Turning Inflation Into Wealth online course, workshops and DVD video course by 2008. (As a mortgage derivatives expert, Mr. Amerman also wrote extensively in 2007 and 2008 about the dangers posed by mortgage derivatives in a time of greed when Wall Street was taking enormous risks, and how that could bring down the financial system in a flash.)

In the years that followed, the workshops in particular provided a double-sided education. Mr. Amerman taught non-traditional investment strategies to audiences of motivated investors, and he in turn learned how to best communicate with audiences that often consisted mostly of self-made millionaires who had made their money in a wide variety of fields. Instead of the dry world of institutional finance and investment analysis books - how to get a highly successful professional or entrepreneur to sit up on the edge of their seat, as he or she put together the pieces for a different approach and new strategies for preserving and expanding the wealth they had built?

The way that the information was presented in the workshops and video courses was refined over the years, even as the extensive data bases and analyses underlying the real estate and gold investment courses were expanded and improved. The end result is the unique information and presentation in The Homeowner Wealth Formula book and series, as well as the extensive underlying research.

Much more information on other research, analyses, books, video courses and workshops is available at:

DanielAmerman.com.

Sources & Methodology Notes

The source for inflation information is the Consumer Price Index for Urban Consumers (CPI-U), as provided by the U.S. Bureau of Labor Statistics (BLS).

The historical 30 year mortgage rates are from Freddie Mac.

Obtaining timely and consistent national real estate statistics can be challenging relative to collecting information on securities such as stocks and bonds, for there is no daily closing price, and price change reporting may be delayed by months as the data is gathered. There are also the issues that where people live changes just a bit each year, as does the year of construction, size and amenities of an average home.

The standard is therefore to use a "pairs-based" methodology, where sales of the same home in different years are used to track real estate price changes, rather than changes in mean or median home prices. This does limit the historical database, with the Freddie Mac House Price Index used in this book going back only to 1975.

The "pairs-based" Case-Schiller index is the norm for media reporting of national housing price movements, however, the most commonly reported measure focuses only on the 20 large metropolitan areas, and these can exhibit very different price behavior than the rest of the country.

The Freddie Mac House Price Index used herein includes all 50 states, as well as the other 300+ metro areas, making it a much better national measure, and it is also based on a pairs methodology which accounts for changes in average home size and amenities over the years. But the national average index slightly changes each year, in a way that is retroactive for all the previous years on the basis of "geographic weighting", which likely primarily reflects estimated population shifts, although Freddie Mac won't release the methodology or the weights.

The data base and analyses used herein were developed over a number of years, and the decision was made to not completely change all prior analyses each time that Freddie Mac decided to retroactively change their index. The index numbers were all accurate at the time that they were downloaded, and they are updated regularly. The earlier years of the index were slightly different for previous years than what Freddie Mac was reporting in 2020, which is likely to be slightly different from the index in 2021, and is likely to be different again in 2022, due to this ongoing retroactive revision of their data base.

The consumer financial information and median home value for 2019 are from the Federal Reserve's 2019 Survey Of Consumer Finances, and do not use a "pairs-based" methodology.

The once per decade median home values from 1940 through 2000 used in Chapter 5 are from the U.S. Census Bureau and do not use a "pairs-based" methodology.

Made in the USA
Columbia, SC
03 April 2021